Thinking of...

Delivering Solutions on the Windows Azure Platform?

Ask the Smart Questions

By Dan Scarfe, Marcus Tillett & Stephen Parker

Copyright ©2009 Dan Scarfe, Marcus Tillett and Stephen Parker

First Published in 2009 by Smart Questions Limited, 8 Loriners Close, Cobham, Surrey, KT11 1BE, UK

Web: *www.Smart-Questions.com* (including ordering of printed and electronic copies, extended book information, community contributions and details on charity donations)

Email: *info@Smart-Questions.com* (for customer services, bulk order enquiries, reproduction requests et al)

The right of Dan Scarfe, Marcus Tillett and Stephen Parker to be identified as the authors of this book has been asserted in accordance with the Copyright, Designs and Patents Act 1998. All rights reserved. No part of this publication may be reproduced, stored in a retrieval system or transmitted, in any form or by any means, electronic, mechanical, recording or otherwise, in any part of the world, without the prior permission of the publisher. Requests for permission should be sent to the publisher at *info@Smart-Questions.com*

Designations used by companies to distinguish their products are often claimed as trademarks. All brand names and product names used in this book are trade names, service marks, trademarks or registered trademarks of their respective owners.

The author and publisher have taken care in preparation of this book, but make no express or implied warranty of any kind and assume no responsibility for errors or omissions. No liability is assumed for incidental or consequential damages in connection with or arising out of the use of the information contained herein.

A catalogue record for this book is available from the British Library.

ISBN 978-0-9561556-3-4

SQ-23-156-001-001

Smart Questions™ Philosophy

Smart Questions is built on 4 key pillars, which set it apart from other publishers:

1. *Smart people want Smart Questions not Dumb Answers*
2. *Domain experts are often excluded from authorship, so we are making writing a book simple and painless*
3. *The community has a great deal to contribute to enhance the content*
4. *We donate a percentage of revenue to a charity voted for by the authors and community. It is great marketing, but it is also the right thing to do*

www.Smart-Questions.com

Reviews

Smart Questions raises the most important considerations for evaluating cloud platforms. With such a fundamental change, there are few simple answers that can be stamped onto every firm. It is more important for IT leaders to consider their own unique environment, and this book provides the tools to conduct that analysis.

Matt Rogers, Director, Global Sales Strategy Windows Azure, Microsoft

www.microsoft.com

If you need an introduction to Azure and you've only got time to read one book, make sure it's this one. I will be recommending it to suits and jeans alike in my organization. It strikes exactly the right balance between the technical and non-technical and is an excellent primer that answers key questions at many levels in a clear and concise manner.

Bert Craven, Enterprise Architect, easyJet

www.easyjet.com

When I was at school, the 3Rs were Reading, wRiting and aRithmetic. Now, for an IT professional thinking about cloud computing, we have a new definition, "Reinforced, Remind and Revealed". Based on an evolving set of the right questions to ask, this book seeks to Reinforce your current model, Remind you of key points and Reveal new insights. Don't start an Azure project without reading this.

Richard Prodger, Technical Director, Active Web Solutions

www.aws.net

The potential of the Cloud is starting to be understood by enterprises. We have been delivering hosted BPM projects to Fortune1000 customers for 5 years, but now customers are asking us to provide long-term production capabilities. Our solutions are based on Microsoft technologies, so Azure seems the perfect platform. However, this is early stages for Azure and the wrong approach would be terminal for Nimbus. By offering questions that we can consider in the context of our business, rather than pre-canned answers, this book has massively de-risked our decision-making process.

Paul Linsell, Founder & CTO, Nimbus

www.nimbuspartners.com

The Windows Azure Platform is a strategic investment for Microsoft and its success is at the heart of our long-term plans. It is critical that we help our partners and customers understand the opportunities that are available, but just as importantly to manage the challenges.

Azure is part of Microsoft's Software plus Services vision, providing partners and customers with the power of choice to deliver applications in the Cloud as well as on-premises. Microsoft wants businesses to invest in Azure because it is the right solution for them, not just because it is new.

The Smart Questions approach provides the questions, both business and technical, that you need to ask yourself so you can successfully take advantage of the power of Azure.

Alistair Beagley, Platform Strategy Advisor, Microsoft

www.microsoft.com

Authors

Dan Scarfe

Co-founder & CEO of Dot Net Solutions Ltd – a Microsoft Gold Certified & managed systems integrator partner based in Windsor, UK. Dan has more than ten years of technical & consulting experience in a variety of sectors & industries. His particular passion is software plus services & evangelizing how rich user experience can provide real additional value to software development projects. He often presents at Microsoft conferences & events & has of late been engaged with the teams in Redmond on Azure and Live Services.

Marcus Tillett

Head of Technology at Dot Net Solutions Ltd, where he currently heads the technical team of architects and developers. Having been building solutions with Microsoft technologies for more than 10 years, his expertise is in software architecture and application development. An evangelist for Microsoft technologies, he is also a pragmatist. He is passionate about understanding and using the latest cutting-edge technology. Prior to joining Dot Net Solutions Ltd, Marcus worked for Atos Origin in the UK. Marcus holds a Ph.D. in NMR spectroscopy from the University of Leicester. Having previously published a number of scientific papers, this is Marcus' first book.

Stephen Parker

A business executive, with over 20 years experience of taking critical technology investment decisions & delivering solutions on the leading edge of IT in large enterprises, '.com' start-ups, & business turnarounds. His recent journey of turning around a struggling ERP vendor into a leading Cloud eProcurement business & taking this to a trade sale has added scars & knowledge in equal measures.

His down to earth approach, backed up by real-life experience & an ability to bridge the gap between board room strategy & the depths of technology, provides him with a rare insight into the world of Cloud Computing. He provides consulting to companies considering Cloud Computing and to analyst firms focused in this space. He is also the author of *Thinking of…Buying a Cloud Solution? Ask the Smart Questions* and *Thinking of…Offering a Cloud Solution? Ask the Smart Questions*.

Acknowledgements

Authors are driven to bring books into existence for a variety of reasons, but there is one common theme: "the support of others". This is our chance to say thank you.

To the team of mainly unsung heroes who have worked long hours to deliver Azure. Without you, there would be no need for this book.

To those who have reviewed the book during its journey to life, providing candid feedback and real world insights.

To our friends and families who have had to put up with late nights and lost weekends. In particular:

Jane;

Vicki and Isobelle;

Elizabeth, Emily and Jonathan.

Table of Contents

1 Major players in IT are spending billions on the Cloud – why? ... 1
2 Could I have a platform in the sky? Sure that'll be $5bn 11
3 Sounds great – let's go? 25
4 Ask the Smart Questions 31
5 What do I need to read? 35
6 Questions for suits 37
7 Questions for jeans 81
8 Funny you should say that 129
9 Time for Action 139
10 Appendix - References 141

Foreword

How hot is cloud computing? The answer is obvious: It's very hot. I'm hard-pressed to think of anything in our industry that's gotten more hype.

How important is cloud computing? That's a harder question to answer. Like all broad innovations, some aspects will matter a lot while others never quite succeed.

On the list of things that will matter a lot, cloud platforms are at the top. Because they let us run applications on low-cost servers while paying only for what we use, cloud platforms are changing how we think about computing.

Of those cloud platforms, it's likely that the Windows Azure Platform will be among the most important. Microsoft's size, market power, and technical acumen all argue in favor of Azure's significance in this area. Anybody who cares about cloud platforms – that is, anybody who cares about IT today – should have at least a basic understanding of the Azure world.

But understanding the Windows Azure Platform means more than just grasping the technology. Cloud platforms like Azure bring new business models, complete with their own benefits and risks. Focusing solely on the technology is myopic – we've got to take a larger view.

A fundamental part of doing this is asking the smart questions, both about the Azure technology and about its business aspects. This book provides an approachable, easy-to-grasp guide to these questions. By looking at both business and technology, it covers the key issues that anybody looking at Azure needs to consider. By doing it in a clear and comprehensible way, it makes these issues easy to get your mind around.

If you're responsible for making decisions about using the Windows Azure Platform, this book is for you.

David Chappell

Principal, Chappell & Associates

Who should read this book?

People like you and me

Although covering a leading edge area of the IT industry this book is not a technical guide, nor was it ever intended to be. It is aimed squarely at those who need to understand where the Windows® Azure™ Platform (**Azure**) fits within the world of technology and how it can be used to deliver value to businesses.

This book is intended to be a catalyst for action, aimed at a range of people inside your organization. Here are just a few, and why it is relevant to them.

Chief Operations Officer

As with any technology, Azure is simply a tool that can be used to address business requirements. As the COO you will want to understand what the operational impacts of developing solutions using this new offering from Microsoft will be.

Will this be a natural evolution from your current processes, or will you need to consider a radical change to how the business operates?

Chief Information Officer/Chief Technical Officer

You have taken time and effort to create a consistent strategy for the use of IT within the business. Now everyone is talking about the Cloud and how it will open up great new opportunities for delivering solutions.

This book will help you understand whether Azure will compliment this strategy or force a rethink.

Solutions Architect

People look to you to bridge the gap between the business needs and the technical reality. Azure offers potentially significant benefits and opportunities; however it also has some constraints. How much of this is simply a "black box" that you have to accept as-is and how much can you control or influence.

Understanding more about both the business and technical aspects of Azure will enable you to continue to offer the appropriate guidance for the programs of work you are responsible for.

Head of Technology/Product Manager

You have a development team with established skills, who are used to working with certain development environments. There is a development lifecycle that people are used to.

How will Azure impact this? Will you need to retrain or recruit new skills, will you need to reconsider the way that customer requests can be built into the product, or how frequently you can offer a new release?

How to use this book

This book is intended to be the catalyst for action. We hope that the ideas and examples inspire you to act. So, do whatever you need to do to make this book useful. Use Post-it notes, photocopy pages, scan pages, and write on it. Go to our website and email colleagues the e-book summary. Rip it apart, or read it quickly in one sitting. Whatever works for you. We hope this becomes your most dog-eared book.

Clever clogs – skip to the questions

Some of you will have a deeper understanding of the background to the Windows Azure Platform and Cloud Computing in general. You may have a pretty good grasp of the implications, benefits and risks. Therefore you may wish to skip to Chapter 4 where the structure of Smart Questions is explained.

But before you go, please read "Getting Involved" on the next page. You can always come back to Chapters 1-3 later.

Getting Involved

The Smart Questions community

There may be questions that we should have asked but didn't. Or specific questions which may be relevant to your situation, but not everyone in general. Go to the website for the book and post the questions. You never know, they may make it into the next edition of the book. That is a key part of the Smart Questions Philosophy.

Send us your feedback

We love feedback. We prefer great reviews, but we'll accept anything that helps take the ideas further. We welcome your comments on this book.

We'd prefer email, as it's easy to answer and saves trees. If the ideas worked for you, we'd love to hear your success stories. Maybe we could turn them into 'Talking Heads'-style video or audio interviews on our website, so others can learn from you. That's one of the reasons why we wrote this book. So talk to us.

feedback@Smart-Questions.com

Got a book you need to write?

Maybe you are a domain expert with knowledge locked up inside you. You'd love to share it and there are people out there desperate for your insights. But you don't think you are an author and don't know where to start. Making it easy for you to write a book is part of the Smart Questions Philosophy.

Let us know about your book idea, and let's see if we can help you get your name in print.

potentialauthor@Smart-Questions.com

Chapter 1

Major players in IT are spending billions on the Cloud – why?

Judge a man by his questions rather than by his answers.
Voltaire (French philosopher, 1694 – 1778)

THE world is changing around us. Users are increasingly becoming used to IT anywhere and everywhere. People are becoming governed and beholden to information systems more than at any point in history. There is an increasing need for access to data wherever a user happens to be and whatever device they are using.

This need for ubiquitous access creates a requirement for more and more processing capacity on a global scale. Organizations are being forced to reconsider how they deliver IT and its underlying infrastructure.

Computing goes through trends in the same way that fashion does. What is state of the art soon becomes legacy and obsolete. What's interesting though is that although the implementations differ and evolve the central ideas and concepts live on and are reborn. There have been a number of incarnations of design for information systems over the years.

The first was centralized IT provided by mainframes. Central servers with all the computing power, delivered user interfaces and data directly to dumb terminals. The advantage of this approach was full control over how the applications were displayed and the data managed. The disadvantage was that the user experience left a lot to be desired and users were beholden to the central IT department.

Desktop software, in particular Microsoft Windows, had great success in the post mainframe era. It delivered software which was easy to use and looked (at the time) great. It had access to the local hardware rather than trying to share a central server with hundreds of users. Each person had a dedicated computer to themselves.

It was easy to write desktop applications for Windows and was cost effective. On the downside, it became increasingly difficult to keep track of data scattered across a myriad of devices and installing software became an administrative nightmare. However, users loved the freedom that their own "local" computer provided.

In the late nineties the Internet and in particular the World Wide Web exploded on to the scene. More and more software moved off the desktop and in to the browser. Now users loved the ability to access their data wherever they were and could run software without needing to install it. The web was the new mainframe, only rather than closed local networks it operated over the Internet.

And here we are today

For many years, the web has enjoyed large success. Of late, however, it has become afflicted by exactly the same issues as the original mainframe. Because the software was executing on a server far removed from the users, performance started to become an issue. Although web based software designers have attempted to rectify this through the use of AJAX, or client-side JavaScript, it only just about achieved the performance of original desktop applications. Another major problem was the myriad of different vendors and versions of browser. This meant it became more and more time consuming and expensive to write web-based software.

The Cloud is the fourth big revolution in IT with Software plus Services being Microsoft's take on what it means. It takes the best parts of the last two revolutions and combines them into one.

What users loved about desktop software was the performance and user experience. What they liked about the web was the availability of centralized data and the reduced need to install software. The Cloud takes data that needs to be centrally stored away from the desktop. It then presents this data in a form, which can be consumed by any application on any device. Data that needs to be stored locally still can be. Microsoft calls this, the power of choice. A user or a developer can pick the most appropriate place to store data and the most effective mechanism to present it to users. Mobile phone software will run on the device, whereas business applications will be delivered via a mix of software running on the device or in a browser. It offers a range of possibilities and alternatives rather than simply enforcing that all data must be stored in the Cloud and all data must be presented via a browser. It seems to make perfect sense and manufacturers such as Apple have embraced it with their iPhone.

Apple runs software on the device and has this software connect to Cloud services to retrieve data. Users still have the benefit of their data being available anywhere without the poor user experience associated with being caged inside a browser. Platforms such as Twitter have shown that it is the application programming interface (API) that is king not the browser. Most power users of Twitter use TweetDeck or other desktop software to manage their streams. The browser is just not powerful enough. Only time will tell whether the web or the Cloud will win, but many are saying the writing is on the wall for an exclusively web-based approach.

What do all the terms mean?

Your customers and end users are confused by the plethora of terms surrounding these new concepts: 'The Cloud', 'Cloud Computing', 'Infrastructure-as-a-Service' 'Platform-as-a-Service', 'Cloud Services', 'Software-as-a-Service' and 'Software plus Services'. These are terms driven by the IT industry and before mass acceptance at the customer level can happen, a generic and simplistic term will have to gain traction. However all these terms mean something unique and describe different things from an IT perspective. If your company is thinking of launching a new product or service it's vital you gain a firm understanding of what each of these different terms mean, what different incarnations are available and ultimately if they are something for you. In the next few sections, each will be described.

'The Cloud'

> The Cloud as a metaphor for the Internet in cloud computing, based on how it is depicted in computer network diagrams and as an abstraction for the complex infrastructure it conceals.
>
> Wikipedia[1]

The Cloud at its simplest level just means the Internet. If you have been involved with software it is something you will know well. It is the symbol you will see in virtually any architecture diagram and generally represents any part of the solution that crosses physical locations.

The term has been seized upon by marketers as a generic term used to describe this new evolution in computing. It is the term that members of the public will most likely have heard of.

Cloud Computing

> Cloud computing is a paradigm of computing in which dynamically scalable and often virtualized resources are provided as a service over the Internet. Users need not have knowledge of, expertise in, or control over the technology infrastructure in the "cloud" that supports them.
>
> Wikipedia[2]

Cloud Computing is one component of The Cloud and is something which has come about, largely because of another major advancement in computing – virtualization. Virtualization is a technology taken into the mainstream by VMware, although Microsoft is now a major player in this area with its Hyper-V technology.

Virtualization is a mechanism whereby a physical server can be divided into a number of 'virtual' servers. A virtual server is a server within a server. Traditionally when you wanted a new server you would need to install the operating system, either directly from a DVD or over the network and install drivers for the physical hardware. It was generally a time consuming and labor intensive process.

---

[1] http://en.wikipedia.org/wiki/The_Cloud

[2] http://en.wikipedia.org/wiki/Cloud_computing

With virtualization, you have the ability to create new servers by simply copying files to a physical server and then starting the virtual machine. With this approach some very interesting possibilities appear. What if we could have hundreds of thousands of physical host servers waiting for virtual machines to be copied to them, which in turn could be instantly booted? What if we could automate this whole process and remove humans from the equation? Today we have this and it is called Cloud Computing.

Cloud Computing is a term that refers to the ability to provision and make available servers, or compute capacity, on demand. It means that you can rent this capacity on an hourly basis. This concept is also described as 'Utility Computing'. You rent as much capacity as you need at any one point in time, much like you pay for as much electricity as you happen to need at a particular time based on the number of household appliances or lights which are currently switched on.

What Cloud Computing gives you is the ability to scale up or scale down the number of servers running your service. This means you don't need to invest in lots of physical equipment which you may or may not need. It takes a lot of the capital risk out of launching your new product or service.

Infrastructure-as-a-Service

> Infrastructure as a Service (IaaS) is the delivery of computer infrastructure (typically a platform virtualization environment) as a service.
> Wikipedia[3]

Infrastructure-as-Service ('IaaS') is the most basic implementation of Cloud Computing.

IaaS provides the ability to host and run virtual servers within a vendor's data centers. The vendor will provide users with the ability to upload a virtual hard drive ('VHD') file and it will then control placing this file on a physical host and setting the configuration according to the user's requirements for their virtual server.

By using an IaaS vendor, users have the ability to create additional copies (instances) of their virtual servers on demand. The data

---
[3] *http://en.wikipedia.org/wiki/Infrastructure_as_a_service*

centers will automatically provision these additional servers, set up firewalls and give you the ability to spread your load across them. You can log on to each individual server and see its desktop and hard drives.

> There are a number of IaaS vendors. The best known is Amazon's Elastic Compute Cloud (*http://aws.amazon.com/ec2/*). EC2 provides a scalable platform for developers to host virtual machines in the Cloud. Others in this space include GoGrid (*www.gogrid.com*), 3Tera (*www.3tera.com*) and Elastic Hosts (*www.elastichosts.com*)

Crucially though, IaaS is just a way to manage and provision virtual servers. Users are still responsible for managing these servers, such as installing updates for the operating system or other software that is installed on them. Users are still responsible for copying their own applications and services on to these servers. Users are also responsible for managing updates to each server individually.

Platform-as-a-Service

> Platform as a service (PaaS) is the delivery of a computing platform and solution stack as a service. It facilitates deployment of applications without the cost and complexity of buying and managing the underlying hardware and software layers.
>
> Wikipedia[4]

Platform-as-a-Service ('PaaS') is an evolution of IaaS. To understand what it means you first need to understand how modern software is written.

Modern software is written and executed using runtimes and frameworks. These provide a lot of the low-level functionality required to access and utilize aspects of the computer's hardware. They are a layer of abstraction between the operating system and the software.

To install your application on a server that has the correct runtime and framework already installed you just compile your code and copy it on to the physical server.

The advantage of a PaaS solution over an IaaS solution is that the operating system is managed by the vendor.

---

[4] *http://en.wikipedia.org/wiki/Platform_as_a_service*

> The Windows Azure Platform is a PaaS. Other major vendors providing this capability are Google and SalesForce. Google has its App Engine (*http://code.google.com/appengine/*) which provides hosting of Python or Java based applications. Force.com (*www.force.com*) from SalesForce provides a proprietary application development and hosting platform.

With a PaaS vendor, at a basic level, rather than just provisioning servers the vendor provisions servers with a runtime environment and framework installed. That is the 'platform'. This means the vendor can now automatically copy your code on to these servers as well. By doing this PaaS vendors can take hardware virtualization and turn it into something which could be described as software virtualization. Rather than provisioning servers you are provisioning blocks of working code; including websites or web services for example.

Cloud Services

> A cloud service includes "products, services and solutions that are delivered and consumed in real-time over the Internet"
> Wikipedia[5]

A Cloud Service is a piece of software that is provided to users over the Internet. They are hosted within a vendor's data center.

Cloud Services are typically used for storing data, user information or performing low level computing operations. Cloud Services publish an application programming interface ('API') and are typically accessed from within applications. Many do have their own web interface which users can interact with which in turn calls the underlying Cloud services.

> Examples of Cloud Services include Flickr (*www.flikr.com*) which provides photo hosting services and MobileMe (*www.apple.com/mobileme/*) which provides centralized services to manage email, contacts and calendars.

Any information stored by a Cloud service can be retrieved from any piece of software running on any device on the Internet.

---

[5] *http://en.wikipedia.org/wiki/Cloud_services#Service*

Software-as-a-Service

> Software as a Service (SaaS, typically pronounced 'sass') is a model of software deployment whereby a provider licenses an application to customers for use as a service on demand.
>
> Wikipedia[6]

Generally, SaaS applications are Cloud-based and delivered via a browser. SaaS vendors normally offer companies some degree of customization to their instance of the application. However the level of customization is controlled by the vendor.

> Examples of SaaS providers include Microsoft's Business Productivity Online Suite *(www.microsoft.com/online/products.mspx)* which provides hosted email, calendar and collaboration and SalesForce (*www.salesforce.com*) which provides hosted customer relationship management.

Software plus Services

> Software plus Services describes the idea of combining hosted services with capabilities that are best achieved with locally running software. It describes composite applications created by combining traditional software with remote services to provide consistent and seamlessly integrated user experience across devices and form factors.
>
> Wikipedia[7]

Software plus Services ('S+S') is Microsoft's vision of computing for the coming years.

Whilst some vendors say the future is almost exclusively Cloud and browser based, Microsoft takes a more pragmatic viewpoint. It is likely Cloud Computing and Cloud Services will play an increasingly important part in architecting tomorrow's information systems and services. However, according to Microsoft, solutions will continue to be comprised of a mix of information stored in the Cloud, information stored on-premises and information stored on devices. Applications will continue to be delivered both through a browser and natively on devices.

---

[6] *http://en.wikipedia.org/wiki/Software_as_a_service*

[7] *http://en.wikipedia.org/wiki/Software_plus_services*

> **Terminology**
>
> We like saving paper. From here on in rather than using the term "Windows® Azure™ Platform", which you will get very bored of reading over and over, we will just use the term "Azure" when referring to it. Where we need to refer to specific components of the platform such as "Windows Azure" we will use the full name.
>
> From here on we have generally used the term "application" to refer to the solution you are building / porting. Where we use the term "system" we are generally talking about integration and referring to existing applications or third party solutions.
>
> "The Cloud" is used as a generic term to refer to the industry as a whole rather than Azure itself.
>
> We use the terms "VM" and "instance" interchangeably. Both refer to a single instance of a role running within Windows Azure.

What does this mean to me?

Cloud computing is firmly upon us. Like every new advance in application development and delivery everyone is keen to understand what it means to their business. If you are a startup or an established company and you are thinking of launching a new product or service, it seems to present a compelling value proposition. It is all too easy, however, to be taken in by the latest fad – especially when the technicians around us present it as the obvious, or sometimes the only option available to us.

We also need to be careful to recognize that whilst this new Cloud model presents potentially attractive business and technical opportunities, it comes with its own set of challenges. On a global scale the issues of physical geographic location of services, varying local legal frameworks, security, reliability and disaster recovery will place a real emphasis on the quality and design of the delivery infrastructure - and this will not come cheap.

Major players in IT are spending billions on the Cloud – why?

Chapter 2

Could I have a platform in the sky? Sure that'll be $5bn

Money frees you from doing things you dislike. Since I dislike doing nearly everything, money is handy.

Groucho Marx (Actor, 1890 - 1977)

MANY still paint a picture of Microsoft as a vendor stuck in the desktop world. They think of Microsoft as selling Windows and Office. Whilst it is true that these products still make up a large part of Microsoft's revenues, the reality is that Microsoft always has been and always will be a platform company.

Microsoft's success with operating systems came not from the software itself but the applications that were written for it. Although Microsoft had its flagship software Office running on the platform, for many years businesses used it because it was the platform of choice for other companies to build software. If you ran Windows, you had the largest choice of third party software available to you. In the last ten years Microsoft has extended this reach from the desktop to the server. Once a realm untouched by them Windows Server now runs on around 70% of servers globally. This success was fuelled once again not by the operating system itself but the range of software that ran on top of it.

Around the same time, Microsoft released a new software development framework, .NET, which ran on its desktop and server operating systems. Somewhere near 50% of all software is now built on top of this platform. ASP.NET is the portion of the platform that is used for creating web software. Although the sands were shifting inside the marketplace, Microsoft was there behind the scenes powering large parts of it.

Many might claim The Cloud is the death knell of the company. The reality is it just presents an excellent opportunity for Microsoft to fully realign itself as a platform company. Rather than the platform solely being for desktops and servers under a customer's control, a new platform in the Cloud was needed.

The investments required to deliver the infrastructure for the Cloud Computing vision are huge[8]. There are very few companies with the funding and vision to deliver this – Microsoft is one of them.

How did Azure come about?

Bill Gates has built one of the most successful software companies in history. His original vision for Windows and his famous 1995 memo led the company through to domination of large parts of information technology. Despite this success, Gates wanted to be remembered for more than just Microsoft. His new passion is his philanthropic work and the Bill and Melinda Gates Foundation[9]. Microsoft needed a new visionary. Microsoft needed a new person to lead them through the rollercoaster ride of IT. They found that person in Ray Ozzie.

Ozzie's first major success was forming Iris Associates, which created what would later become Lotus Notes. Several years after IBM acquired Lotus he left to form Groove Networks, which developed an enterprise collaboration tool[10]. Although the significance of Groove was easy to miss it was one of the first generation of Software plus Services solutions. Gates knew this was the direction the company had to take and Ozzie took up the reigns.

---

[8] That said history has shown us that new entrants with little money can fundamentally change a market, invalidating previously accepted business and financial models.

[9] http://www.gatesfoundation.org

[10] http://en.wikipedia.org/wiki/Ray_Ozzie

Could I have a platform in the sky? Sure that'll be $5bn

The Exchange, Vista and Office 2007 launch was Gates' last big fanfare. Away from the fanfare, deep inside Microsoft, plans were being hatched. Big plans. Ozzie knew that if Microsoft was to continue to occupy the dominant position it did whilst Gates was in charge Microsoft needed to come out blazing. The Software plus Services marketing message and project Red Dog were born.

Red Dog would be a herculean project. Amitabh Srivastava, a Senior VP, was tasked with the job. What was needed was to pull together every major Server and management asset Microsoft owned and create a monstrous Cloud Platform.

Microsoft had the tools for the job. Windows Server and Hyper-V provided an excellent bedrock. The physical servers are managed by System Center. Virtual machines can then be placed, run and managed through the same interface. System Center can be managed programmatically, allowing a living, breathing fabric to be created. Layer on top of this a suite of services and SQL Server and you have a compelling proposition.

The scale of what was created was enormous and is called the Windows Azure Platform.

> The Azure brand, according to folklore, was first coined by Amitabh himself. When at a local DIY store he was looking for paint to create a cloud scene on the roof of his bathroom. Azure was the blue for the sky he needed and named Microsoft's Cloud after it. The authors can neither confirm nor deny the truth of this story.
>
> The brand has been through a number of iterations. When first launched it was described as the "Azure Services Platform" before being rebranded as the Windows Azure Platform.
>
> Other components have been through variants as well, with SQL Azure starting out as SQL Server Data Services, then SQL Data Services, followed by just SQL Services before arriving at its final name. .NET Services has had less interference from the marketing department with just one previous name - BizTalk Services.

How big are we talking?

Big. Very big.

The physical infrastructure requirements to deliver an enterprise-class Cloud platform are mind boggling. First, we need servers, hundreds of thousands of servers. Data centers are needed to house these servers. Enormous data centers. The Chicago, Illinois facility covers over 700,000 square feet – approximately the size of

Could I have a platform in the sky? Sure that'll be $5bn

16 American football fields — with critical power of 60 megawatts — enough to power 40,000 homes. The Dublin facility is 303,000 square feet and power will reach 22.2 mega watts critical power.

Chicago data center

However constructing these mega-data centers was becoming increasingly challenging. Normal data centers are full of servers divided into aisles of server cabinets. Technicians could replace failed servers and components with ease. The problem with this approach is that the space requirements are colossal. This in turn makes cooling more difficult.

Generation four (Gen 4)[11] data centers are a radical approach to address these issues. Instead of arranging servers in large rooms, they are packed in an ultra-dense format inside shipping containers. So dense there is only enough room for connecting wires and dedicated cooling between the servers. Typical server density is ten times that of traditional data centers. Each container includes 1,800 to 2,500 servers and once full, they are welded shut. Two-thirds of the Chicago data center is optimized for housing containerized servers.

Dublin data center

A typical data center runs a power usage effectiveness[12] (PUE) of 2.5. PUE is determined by dividing the amount of power entering a data center by the power used to run the computer infrastructure within it. PUE is therefore expressed as a ratio, with overall efficiency improving as the quotient decreases toward 1. By utilizing Gen 4 design Microsoft is able to deliver a yearly average

---

[11] http://loosebolts.wordpress.com/2008/12/02/our-vision-for-generation-4-modular-data-centers-one-way-of-getting-it-just-right/

[12] http://www.microsoft.com/environment/our_commitment/articles/green_grid.aspx

calculated at 1.22. This is leagues ahead of power efficiencies delivered by traditional data centers.

The shipping containers are delivered to the data center, sat next to one another and power and fiber optic cables connected. If a server inside the container fails, it is simply marked as if it were a bad sector on a disk. Once the container suffers too many failed servers it is unplugged, removed and swapped with another.

Once you have the ability to create data centers quickly and simply you can create lots of them. Microsoft has plans to create facilities around the world at the cost of roughly $500m each.

What's in the kit bag?

Microsoft is somewhat late with a Cloud offering. Rivals such as Amazon are more established in the market. However, by observing rivals and investing over $5bn, the set of services and capabilities that Microsoft are bringing to the party are impressive. The Windows Azure Platform is a PaaS within the definitions used in Chapter 1.

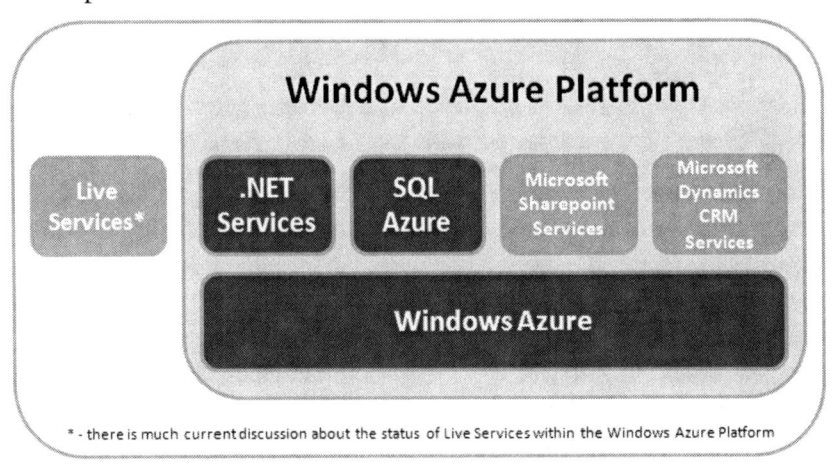

Windows Azure Platform

- Live Services*
- .NET Services
- SQL Azure
- Microsoft Sharepoint Services
- Microsoft Dynamics CRM Services

Windows Azure

* - there is much current discussion about the status of Live Services within the Windows Azure Platform

The key constituent parts of the platform are outlined below:

Windows Azure

Windows Azure is the core of the Windows Azure Platform. It is effectively an operating system that runs the data centers. Providing the basic building blocks for a platform as a service – compute, storage and management.

Could I have a platform in the sky? Sure that'll be $5bn

Compute Service

The primary purpose of a Cloud computing platform is to host and execute applications. Windows Azure is primarily targeted at applications requiring global scale, applications that have varying requirements for compute capacity or scenarios where companies do not have the infrastructure skills required to manage the underlying servers. That said, there are a number of other scenarios where Azure can offer real benefits. Microsoft has a stated goal of moving its large-scale applications such as Hotmail on to the platform.

A key tenet of Cloud computing is the ability to scale applications in line with demand. There are two mechanisms for achieving this scaling. Scale up means hosting your application on ever larger and more powerful servers. Scale-out means hosting on a greater number of low-power commodity servers. Windows Azure provides massive scale-out capabilities.

The scale-out is achieved by providing the ability to provision an effectively unlimited number of virtual machine (VM) instances. These VMs run 64-bit Windows Server 2008. The VMs are executed by a modified version of Microsoft's Hyper-V technology.

Each provisioned VM is classified as providing one instance of a role. There are a number of roles, at present, these include:

The web role is primarily responsible for accepting HTTP connections and responding to these requests. Web roles can also be used to perform basic calculations. Web roles run on IIS 7 and can execute .NET code, such as ASP.NET or WCF. Additionally web roles provide FastCGI support allowing PHP applications to be executed. Support for Python and Ruby will also be included when the platform launches.[13]

The worker role is designed to undertake background processing work. Work can be passed to worker roles via Windows Azure Queues. A worker can also make outbound connections to a service that could provide it with work to do.

---

[13] *http://www.microsoft.com/azure/whatisazure.mspx*

Each role runs an agent. This agent allows the role to report its health to the Windows Azure management fabric along with logging and sending alerts.

As part of a solution, developers can use a mix of any number of each kind of role.

One important aspect to consider is that developers do not have access to upload custom VM images, nor do they get direct access to the underlying operating system and should make no assumptions about it. This is in sharp contrast to IaaS providers such as Amazon.

Storage Service

Data is an integral part of any application. Providing mechanisms to persist and transfer this information is vital for any Cloud platform. Windows Azure provides a number of methods to achieve this. SQL Azure also provides data storage and is discussed separately below. All data stored within Windows Azure is triple-replicated. All data is made available using standard REST calls. Within .NET developers can make use of ADO.NET Data Services, although this is not required. Other environments can make RESTful HTTP requests.

Blob Service

The Blob service is the simplest form of storage and is not dissimilar to the file system on a hard drive. Each account is comprised of a number of containers, which are a bit like folders. Blobs can be stored within each container. A blob might be a document, picture or MP3. Each blob can be up to 50GB in size and can have additional information (metadata) associated with it.

The Blob service includes support for taking a large file and uploading it piece by piece. This means if there is a network connectivity issue during upload individual failed pieces can be resent instead of the whole file.

Table Service

For more complex data storage requirements, Windows Azure provides the Table Service. It's easy to be confused by the name into thinking this is a database in the Cloud. Data stored within the Table Service is held as a series of entities that have associated properties. For example, if you wanted to store information about

Could I have a platform in the sky? Sure that'll be $5bn

a user you would be able to specify that a user had a name and email address - a classic PropertyBag implementation. The entity has a flexible schema, meaning that two "user" entities can have different properties. The available data types for a property are limited.

Some developers will find it foreign to store large amounts of data within this format. There is a very good reason though: scalability. With the Table service, it is possible to store billions of entities comprising petabytes of data.

To enable this scaling the Table Service has the concept of partitions. A partition is a logical grouping of records. Windows Azure can place each partition on a different physical server. The smaller the number of records within a partition (and therefore the higher the number of partitions) the better the storage will scale. There are a number of tradeoffs surrounding this, which are discussed in greater depth in Chapter 7.

Queue Service

The queuing mechanism within Windows Azure is one of the vital components that enable work to be scaled-out. Different portions of work can be handed out to different servers, allowing load to be spread as demand increases.

Take making a drink in your favorite coffee house. Some coffee houses will have a barista taking your order and then making your drink themselves. The problem this leaves is that it's impossible to alter the ratio of order takers to order makers. Other coffee houses will have servers taking the order, writing them on the cup and then placing them in a queue for the baristas to make. By doing this, team members can be deployed as either order takers or baristas depending on whether there is a queue for service or for drinks to be made.

Queuing within Windows Azure is the same. A message can be placed onto a queue to be picked up by e.g. a worker role. This message might be an instruction to resize a photo, or connect to another system. The work needs to be a defined task that can be completed without asking additional questions of whatever instigated the task.

Fabric

Data centers contain a variety of physical equipment, including servers, switches and load balancers that collectively are called the fabric. Managing all of these assets is the job of the Fabric Controller. This software is the brains of the Windows Azure Platform.

Each application deployed on Windows Azure includes an XML configuration file. This file includes information such as the number of each kind of role required. The Fabric Controller uses this information to automatically provision the correct number of VMs and installs the application on to them. The Fabric Controller is responsible for ensuring physical servers are fully utilized yet not overloaded.

As part of this provisioning the Fabric Controller identifies and enforces fault domains. A fault domain may be servers in a particular container, a particular switch or a particular power distribution unit. It will always ensure that there is never a situation where all the roles for a particular application are within a single fault domain. This means if, for example, a switch were to fail there would always be another instance connected to a different switch that would continue to operate.

The Fabric Controller is also responsible for maintaining the health of the fabric. The Fabric Controller can communicate with the agent on each role to determine its heath. This gives it a real-time view of the state of the fabric. If a role fails, a replacement is automatically instantiated.

Finally, the Fabric Controller is responsible for maintaining the software on the VMs. This includes installing operating system updates, framework updates or security fixes, as well as the deployment of your applications. Through the use of update domains the Fabric Controller will ensure that all the roles executing the application are never all updated simultaneously. This ensures there will always be a number of roles active.

Could I have a platform in the sky? Sure that'll be $5bn

Pricing[14]

Compute	$0.12/hour
Storage	$0.15/GB/month
	plus $0.01/10k storage transactions
Bandwidth	$0.10/GB ingress (inbound)
	$0.15/GB egress (outbound)

SLAs

>99.95% guarantee that your service is connected and reachable via the web (assuming a minimum of 2 of each kind of role).

>99.9% guarantee the storage service will be available/reachable and that storage requests will be processed successfully.

.NET Services

When writing any application there is a base level of functionality required – compute and storage – which is provided by Windows Azure. In addition to this, there are other common requirements, such as message exchange and authentication & authorization. .NET Services provides a number of these building-block infrastructure services. These services can be used by either Cloud-based or on-premises applications. New capabilities are being added on a regular basis[15] and in time there will be a suite of functionality within .NET Services, but for now it is comprised of two key pieces.

Access Control Service

Users are often required to manage multiple usernames and passwords. This is due to the number of identity providers commonly used today. These include Windows Live ID, Google, FaceBook and corporate Active Directories. Some applications create their own authentication and authorization solutions. This can result in problems as most developer are not security experts. Microsoft's first attempt to solve this challenge was the much-

---

[14] All prices are correct at the time of publication, but subject to change

[15] *http://blogs.msdn.com/netservices/archive/2009/09/18/update-on-the-next-microsoft-net-services-ctp.aspx*

maligned Project Hailstorm (aka Passport). This approach failed, partly, because it tried to create a single identity provider.

Recently, there has been a move towards a claims-based identity model. The Access Control Service uses this model to allow an application to delegate authentication and authorization. The Access Control Service can process a claim from an issuing identity provider. It can then apply rules, which developers can configure, to determine what parts of an application users are given access to and what they can do once there.

The Access Control Service supports the WS-Trust 1.3 protocol and creates SAML (Security Assertion Markup Language) compliant security tokens. It provides familiar integration for developers using REST, SOAP and WCF bindings.

Service Bus

Microsoft's vision is that applications will continue to be composed of both on-premises and Cloud based components. This necessitates a need to exchange data and messages between applications irrespective of their location.

The Service Bus allows these applications and services to be connected together. It does this by acting as a service intermediary, providing relay and connectivity services. Providing this bidirectional communication between services over the internet would otherwise be challenging. This is because of issues such as network address translation (NAT), dynamic IP addresses and security devices such as firewalls.

The Service Bus utilizes advanced NAT traversal techniques and is based on REST, SOAP and WS-* protocols. It provides familiar integration for developers using WCF bindings. The Service Bus also provides a discovery system for available endpoints through the Service Bus Registry.

Pricing

Messages	$0.15/100k messages
Bandwidth	$0.10/GB ingress (inbound)
	$0.15/GB egress (outbound)

Could I have a platform in the sky? Sure that'll be $5bn

SLA

>99.9% guarantee that the .NET Service Bus endpoint will have external connectivity and that message operation requests will be processed successfully.

SQL Azure

SQL Azure is a relational database in the Cloud. It provides high availability, scalability and resilience. In comparison, Windows Azure Table storage provides a semi-structured data store.

SQL Azure is a major evolution from the SDS version announced at the Professional Developers Conference (PDC) in October 2008. SQL Azure provides the core relational database features and is built on standard SQL Server technologies.

SQL Azure provides the same tabular data stream (TDS) interface as SQL Server. This is the protocol used by many standard client libraries, such as ADO.NET. This means that the same tools and libraries can continue to be used by developers.

SQL Azure supports a subset of the full SQL Server features, including tables, views, indexes, triggers and stored procedures. Currently there is no support for distributed transaction and the CLR, which is required for spatial data types. Microsoft assesses that the current feature set addresses about 95% of web and departmental workloads.

Pricing

Web Edition	$9.99/month (1 GB)
Business Edition	$99.99/month (10 GB)
Bandwidth	$0.10/GB ingress (inbound)
	$0.15/GB egress (outbound)

SLA

>99.9% guarantee of external connectivity.

Commercial availability

At commercial launch Azure will be available in Austria, Belgium, Canada, Denmark, Finland, France, Germany, Ireland, India, Italy, Japan, Netherlands, New Zealand, Norway, Portugal, Spain, Sweden, Switzerland, UK, and the United States. Israel is currently being evaluated. By the March 2010 timeframe it is expected that commercial availability will be expanded to Australia, Brazil, Chile, Colombia, Czech Republic, Greece, Hong Kong, Hungary, Israel, South Korea, Malaysia, Mexico, Poland, Puerto Rico, Romania, Singapore, and Taiwan.[16]

What's the Roadmap?

The Windows Azure Platform will continue to receive substantial investment over the coming years. Microsoft has been very clear that functionality which is not completely finished and enterprise grade will be pushed into later versions. Nothing will be released until it is completely ready. Microsoft only has once chance with Azure and any outages, poor performance or problems will be seized upon by competitors.

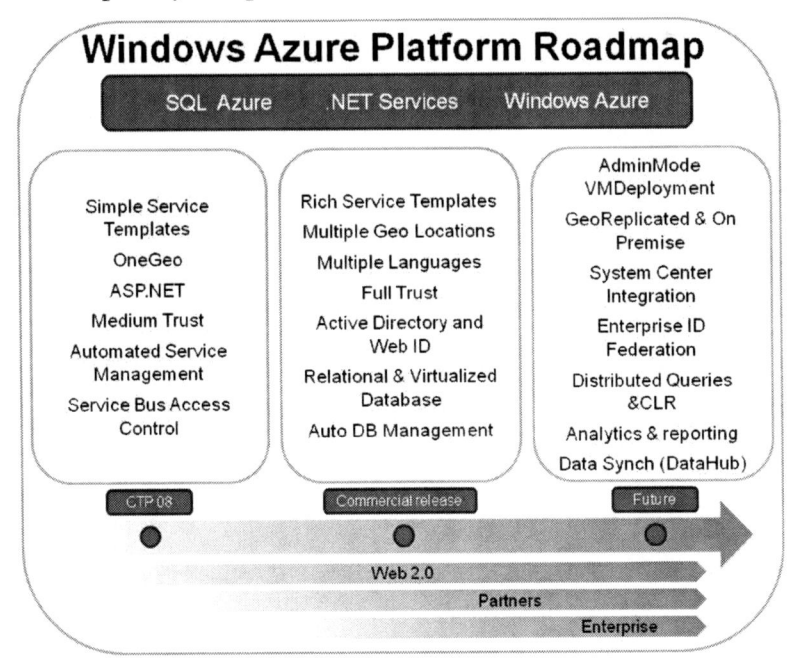

Windows Azure Platform Roadmap

SQL Azure	.NET Services	Windows Azure
Simple Service Templates	Rich Service Templates	AdminMode VMDeployment
OneGeo	Multiple Geo Locations	GeoReplicated & On Premise
ASP.NET	Multiple Languages	System Center Integration
Medium Trust	Full Trust	Enterprise ID Federation
Automated Service Management	Active Directory and Web ID	Distributed Queries & CLR
Service Bus Access Control	Relational & Virtualized Database	Analytics & reporting
	Auto DB Management	Data Synch (DataHub)
CTP 08	Commercial release	Future

Web 2.0
Partners
Enterprise

---

[16] http://www.microsoft.com/azure/faq.mspx

Could I have a platform in the sky? Sure that'll be $5bn

In terms of major pieces of functionality missing at present:

- SharePoint & CRM capabilities are not being included within version 1.
- .NET Services has been relieved of its workflow capabilities until .NET 4.0 is available.
- SQL Azure does not include functionality beyond the basic database engine. Other parts of SQL Server, such as Analysis Services, should arrive soon.

Chapter 3

Sounds great – let's go?

Logical consequences are the scarecrows of fools and the beacons of wise men.
Thomas Huxley (Scientist, 1825 - 1895)

SOME are saying a move to the Cloud is a step as big as the coming of the Internet originally. Certainly if the moves taken since Ray Ozzie has been at Microsoft are anything to go by it is something they are taking very seriously. As we move, socially and culturally, to a more globally connected society it appears to be a logical progression to have computing delivered at a global rather than local level. It is therefore hard to believe that the Cloud and Azure will not become deeply engrained within the future of IT.

Where do I Sign?

So all this sounds great. However, it is important to understand whether you should be one of the leaders or the followers. Many factors will drive how you position your company for this opportunity. There will be benefits and risks. Being clear about both of these will be key to making the correct call. After all Azure is only a piece of technology and it needs to fit with you and your customers business plans.

Sounds great – let's go?

You need a position

It may be the right thing for your company to dive into the Cloud and fully embrace Azure. On the other hand adopting a "watching brief" could be the right approach. However, what you cannot do is have no position at all, bury your head in the sand and hope it all goes away.

How aggressively you define and communicate your position will depend on what is happening in your market. If you are losing business right now, then that is a major motivator to act now. If the analysts are identifying your industry as "ripe for Cloud services" then now might be a good time to start planning.

What is essential is that you actually have a position and clearly communicate it externally and just as importantly internally.

New opportunities

Azure has the potential to open up new market opportunities, to allow you to create dynamic new solutions or to fundamentally change the commercial parameters for your solutions.

However the new opportunities are likely to bring with them new challenges. Do you have the sales and marketing skills to reach out to the new markets? What about the technical skills to develop the new Azure solutions? Do you have the business processes that will allow you to deal with thousands rather than hundreds of customers who are now paying on a monthly rather than annual basis?

The provisioning of the deployment environment is now, largely automated by Azure. If you have staff whose current job is to carry out this role, can you redeploy them to other activities? Can they now carry out more customer facing roles such as training or consulting?

To a large extent these are business and commercial issues rather than technology ones.

New competitors

Just as the Cloud opens up new opportunities for you, it will open up opportunities for others. These may be startups with lower overheads or businesses entering your market for the first time. Can you use your existing experience to differentiate and be a trusted advisor when change is happening all around? Can you create barriers that make it difficult for these new players? Can you learn from them and be more effective yourselves?

New Models

Traditionally there were limited choices when purchasing hardware and software. Hardware has a defined cost based on how powerful the processors are and how redundant each part of it is. Software has an up-front price with an annual support and maintenance cost.

Cloud computing and the Cloud in general opens up such a myriad of choices that it's easy to become overwhelmed and confused.

Commercial

Just because a new model comes out it doesn't automatically mean old models are bad. There's an old adage that "if it ain't broke don't fix it" and this is very often true in IT. Cloud computing will open up a range of new possibilities and solutions to age-old problems. If you don't suffer from any of these problems, your IT function is responsive and you don't find yourself inhibited, then sticking with what you have may be the right choice.

The Cloud hype is all about monthly, annuity billing, but this does not mean that it is the only model. The move to OPEX is seen as a key benefit and moves IT into a place where it can be treated like many other areas of business and outsourced. However, for some companies CAPEX may still be their preferred model.

A single answer is rarely appropriate across an entire business. What Azure offers is choice. These choices may not be ones you want right now. However, the rate of change in the Cloud space means that it would be unwise not to check back on a regular basis.

Technical

When you own the servers you can do as you please. When you are using someone else's platform your degree of control changes.

Sounds great – let's go?

This could be a good thing as it may enforce a discipline of process and organization upon you. Or, it could create such restrictions that you are unable to run critical business processes as required.

Using a Platform as a Service such as Azure also takes you firmly down a defined technology path. Microsoft are however, going to great lengths to be seen as opening up the Azure platform e.g. allowing PHP based code and interoperating with external claims based authentication providers. In any case, many businesses have already standardized on Microsoft so this is simply an extension of that decision.

Maturity

The Cloud as a whole is still relatively immature and Azure itself is brand new. Access to the Cloud is reliant upon reliable internet connectivity, which is itself still maturing and not universally available.

The lessons are being learnt (in many cases the hard way) about how to keep these vast data centers going. Telecommunications providers are bringing higher bandwidth and more reliable connectivity to us all the time.

Does the current state of Cloud maturity allow all business scenarios to be addressed with Cloud solutions? No, and it is likely that this isn't actually a realistic end game anyway. This is why Microsoft are so passionate about the Software + Services message. However the rate at which things are maturing is impressive and areas that may be considered "out of scope" today could be "in scope" tomorrow.

The vast majority of the IT ecosystem (consulting, design, development, support) is still focused on the traditional on-premises world. However, Microsoft is investing in a huge way to skill its partners for this new opportunity. There will also be a self fulfilling process. As more customers want Cloud offerings, so more Azure based applications will be created. This will extend the number of customers who can have their needs met, creating further demand and so on.

Fortune favors the ~~brave~~ prepared

Everything in business has an element of risk associated with it. It is how we prepare for and manage these risks that counts. The Cloud may not be the right thing for you. However making that decision should be made with your eyes wide open, not with your head in the sand with fingers crossed.

Read on for the questions that we trust will help make things a little clearer.

Sounds great – let's go?

Chapter 4

Ask the Smart Questions

If I have seen further it is by standing on the shoulders of giants.
Isaac Newton (Scientist, 1643 – 1727)

SMART Questions is about giving you valuable insights or "the Smarts". Normally these are only gained through years of painful and costly experience. Whether you already have a general understanding of the subject and need to take it to the next level or are starting from scratch, you need to make sure you ask the Smart Questions. We aim to short circuit that learning process, by providing the expertise of the 'giants' that Isaac Newton referred to.

Not all the questions will necessarily be new or staggeringly insightful. The value you get from the information will clearly vary. It depends on your job role and previous experience. We call this the 3Rs.

The 3 Rs

Some of the questions will be in areas where you know all the answers so they will be **Reinforced** in your mind.

You may have forgotten certain areas so the book will **Remind** you.

Other questions may be things you've never considered and will be **Revealed** to you.

How do you use Smart Questions?

The structure of the questions is set out in Chapter 5, and the questions are in Chapters 6 and 7. The questions are laid out in a series of structured and ordered tables with the questions in one column and the explanation of why it matters alongside. We've also provided a checkbox so that you can mark which questions are relevant to your particular situation.

A quick scan down the first column in the list of questions should give you a general feel of where you are for each question vs. the 3Rs.

At the highest level they are a sanity check or checklist of areas to consider. You can take them with you to meetings or use them as the basis of your ITT. Just one question may save you a whole heap of cash or heartache.

In Chapter 8 we've tried to bring some of the questions to life with some real-world examples.

We trust that you will find real insights. There may be some 'aha' moments. Hopefully, not too many sickening, 'head in the hands – what have we done' moments, where you've realized that your company is hopelessly exposed. If you're in that situation, then the questions may help you negotiate yourself back into control.

In this context, probably the most critical role of the questions is that they reveal risks that you hadn't considered. On the flip side they should also open up your thinking to opportunities that you hadn't necessarily considered. Balancing the opportunities and the risks, and then agreeing what is realistically achievable is the key to formulating strategy.

The questions could be used in your internal operational meetings to inform or at least prompt the debate. Alternatively they could shape the discussion you have with potential third party organizations or partners who will assist with your move to Azure.

How to dig deeper

Need more information? Not convinced by the examples, or want ones that are more relevant to you specific situation? The Smart Questions micro-site for the book has a list of other supporting material. As this subject is moving quickly many of the links are to websites or blogs.

There is also a community of people who've read the book and are all at different levels of maturity who have been brought together on the Smart Questions micro-site for the book.

And finally

Please remember that these questions are NOT intended to be a prescriptive list that must be followed slavishly from beginning to end. It is also inevitable that the list of questions is not exhaustive and we are confident that with the help of the community the list of Smart Questions will grow.

If you want to rephrase a question to improve its context or have identified a question we've missed, then let us know so we can add it to the collective knowledge.

We also understand that not all of the questions will apply to all businesses. However, we encourage you to read them all as there may be a nugget of truth that can be adapted to your circumstances.

Above all, we do hope that it provides a guide or a pointer to the areas that may be valuable to you and helps with the "3 Rs"

Chapter 5

What do I need to read?

Any time, any place, anywhere.

Martini drinks advert (1970 – 1980s)

THERE are two main considerations as to whether Azure is suitable for your business and your clients' businesses – business and technical. The questions you need to think about have been divided into these two sections. If you are more technically or operationally focused you can skip the next chapter, however you may want to read on so you know the questions that the business needs to ask.

Please also note that whilst we have tried to provide as wide a coverage of the subject as possible there will inevitably be some questions missing (please let us know *feedback@Smart-Questions.com*). You may also feel that there are too many things to consider and even wonder whether you should just give up. This is certainly not our intention. Our goal is to help you manage risk and understanding the Smart Questions is central to this – there is no such thing as risk avoidance as even doing nothing creates its own risks.

What do I need to read?

The following two chapters of questions are organized in the following way.

Chapter 6: Questions for suits

1. Why are we considering Azure?
2. Is Azure right for my customers?
3. Is Azure right for my business?
4. Commercial considerations?

Chapter 7: Questions for jeans

1. The big picture
2. Design considerations
3. Developing for Azure
4. Application lifecycle management

Chapter 6

Questions for suits

Effective management always means asking the right question.
Robert Heller (Business Management Author)

NO matter how much you are driven by the joy of technology there are still a series of questions that you need to ask to ensure there is a sound business foundation to your decision making process.

Some of the questions will be more relevant to in-house teams with others better suited to independent software vendors (ISVs). However we would encourage you to read all of them as there may be gems hiding in there leading to a "Reveal".

This chapter covers the business focused questions and will help you to understand if a move to Azure is right on a business basis for both you and your customers. However just because you wear a suit does not mean you should ignore the next chapter. It is often helpful to understand what it is like to wear somebody else's clothes. So go on read this chapter and then slip into a pair of jeans and see how it feels.

6.1 Why are we considering Azure?

The Cloud in general and specifically Azure is a radical shift from traditional on-premises based applications. There are a number of great advantages to moving to the Cloud, but there are a number of risks as well.

Having a clear understanding of what has motivated you to get involved with or look at Azure is a key place to start. With this defined other businesses decisions will have greater clarity and focus.

It is all too easy to end up diving in, just because it is new and hope that a plan will become clearer as you progress. You may be able to manage this if Azure is currently an R&D project. But what happens if, somewhere along the way, this has become a "bet the business" leap of faith?

Questions for suits > Why are we considering Azure?

☒	Question	Why this matters
☐	6.1.1 Have you lost business because you did not have a Cloud offering?	There is no more compelling reason to consider alternative approaches than when you are actively losing business. Azure could be a quick route to a Cloud offering. Or the right option might be to explain why the Cloud is not yet right in your sector (security, data location). Whatever the right positioning for you and your sector, it would be more effective if you could present your position as early as possible and establish the intellectual high ground.
☐	6.1.2 Are your customers asking for a move to Cloud Computing?	Even if you have not yet lost business directly a sure sign of things to come is when your customers are talking and asking. You have an opportunity to be ready to have the conversation.
☐	6.1.3 Are your customers looking for a fundamental shift in the cost models for IT?	Your customers, whether in-house departments or 3rd parties, may be under pressure to fundamentally review their cost base for IT. For example a reduction of technical infrastructure staff or a move to OPEX from CAPEX. A Cloud based offering with Azure at its heart may facilitate an answer to these requests.
☐	6.1.4 Are your customers looking to outsource IT?	Businesses outsource many aspects of their operations. There is a growing recognition that there is nothing special about IT preventing it from being considered as well. Cloud offerings can reduce the IT footprint that the customer is responsible for managing. Can your offerings move to Azure and be part of this as well?

Questions for suits > Why are we considering Azure?

☒	Question	Why this matters
☐	6.1.5 Are your existing competitors offering a Cloud solution?	Just as you are now thinking about the Cloud, it is likely that your competitors are as well. You need to be positioned to respond, either with your own offering or with a positive defensive story. However just because defending your current position is the easy option it does not make it the correct one.
☐	6.1.6 Are new suppliers entering your market with a Cloud offering?	One of the reasons for considering the Cloud is that it provides the opportunity to extend your reach either geographically or into other verticals. Unfortunately, just as this is good for you, it also means that other suppliers can extend into your markets. One of the challenges here is that you may not even be aware that these businesses exist never mind that they are competitors.
☐	6.1.7 Are the industry analysts for your sector predicting that now is the right time for the Cloud?	Arguably the first safe time to start your move to the Cloud is when the analysts for your sector are predicting the Cloud. Although you will have missed the early adopter position you will have the benefit of not having spent as much time educating your customers. As always there is a fine balance and each business will have their own style that will determine where this balance point is.
☐	6.1.8 Can you increase the barriers of entry for potential competitors?	Although the Cloud is often seen as something that is reducing barriers to entry, it may be that in your sector the reverse is true. Can you create patents that lock out or make it difficult for your competitors (or new entrants) to follow you? Does Azure provide flexibility that others cannot match?

Questions for suits > Why are we considering Azure?

☒	Question	Why this matters
☐	6.1.9 Does the Cloud present a Blue Ocean Strategy[17] opportunity?	A Blue Ocean Strategy has at its heart the notion of making your competitors strengths irrelevant by providing the customer with something so different that you change the game. For example, the Nintendo Wii has been successful because it did not compete with Sony and Microsoft for the hard core gamer, but offered a console that the other 90+% of the population could enjoy. The strengths of the PlayStation and Xbox were irrelevant to these new gamers. Has the Cloud the potential to do this for you?
☐	6.1.10 Will it give you competitive advantage?	Being seen as offering a Cloud solution may in itself enhance the market's perception of you. It may be part of your business model to be seen as leading edge. Any change is an opportunity to create differentiation and establish advantage in the market. Connecting to Microsoft's move to the Cloud with Azure may further enhance your positioning.
☐	6.1.11 Is your reputation based on being bleeding edge, so this is just what you do?	You may have built your reputation both with customers and employees of always being on the leading edge. Working in this space creates marketing and publicity opportunities and right now Azure is one of the most "in focus" areas within Microsoft.

---

[17] *Blue Ocean Strategy* by W. Chan Kim & Renee Mauborgne

Questions for suits > Why are we considering Azure?

☒	Question	Why this matters
☐	6.1.12 Are you perceived as safe, and want to add a little edge to your offerings?	Although the marketing noise is always about the latest greatest thing, the reality is that most businesses are run on last year's technologies. Most companies are conservative by nature and hence you may have established a great reputation as the safe trusted advisor. Azure may be a low risk way to add a Cloud element to your offerings and create a little edge. However, make sure that this is based first and foremost on offering value to your customers in the safe way they expect. Remember for these customers the Cloud is probably a bonus rather than the raison d'etre for buying.
☐	6.1.13 Are you in a desperate place and need to do something radical?	Are you in trouble, investors ready to close down the business and you need something radical to continue? This is a tough place to be. However provided your investors and staff are clear about the risks and costs involved it may be a great way to reinvent the business[18]. The key is not to throw out all of your business experience, there are still real customers who need offerings to real issues and there needs to be a sound business plan. There are the headlines about businesses that have no current revenue streams and yet have multi-million dollar valuations – remember these are NOT the norm.

---

[18] This was IMPAQ Business Solutions story, with a happy trade-sale ending

Questions for suits > Why are we considering Azure?

☒	Question	Why this matters
☐	6.1.14 Can you address new markets?	With the reach of the internet can you offer your solutions to geographies outside your home base? Although many of the traditional barriers to entry may be reduced, you may still need to consider partnering with local companies to provide local sales support, training or on-site consulting. Also consider the positive impact of Azures geo-located data centers.
☐	6.1.15 Can you address new industry verticals?	Can you work with a larger customer base across related industry verticals by offering multiple configurable variants on your core product? A single code base deployed via the Azure Platform, but configurable to meet the needs of differing verticals could open up new opportunities.
☐	6.1.16 Is the physical ability to provision your on-premises infrastructure requirements a barrier for some customers?	In some situations it may not be possible to provide the infrastructure for the servers, storage and networking to make your offerings work. Are there also considerations about the technical skills to keep it working? For example, could a ruggedized laptop with satellite communication that connects to the core infrastructure on Azure, remove the need for local infrastructure and open up new customer opportunities?
☐	6.1.17 Are the costs associated with your on-premises infrastructure a barrier for some customers?	Although your customer may have the infrastructure and skills are they happy to pay for the server farm required to provide reasonable response times? Especially if there is a low average utilization. Can the Azure "Pay as you go" model help break this barrier?

43

Questions for suits > Why are we considering Azure?

☒	Question	Why this matters
☐	6.1.18 Can Azure help remove barriers associated with processing power and scale?	You may have a very processing intensive part of your offering that requires large hardware capabilities to provide reasonable response times. However for most of the time this infrastructure is un-used. Has this created barriers both around the costs to the customer to deploy this infrastructure, but also in your ability to scale with the customer's needs? The flexible charge models for use of Azure processing may make a move to Azure the right move for you.
☐	6.1.19 Will the Cloud help reduce your support costs related to product versions?	It maybe that many of the calls to your helpdesk are for issues that have already been solved with more recent releases. However because the customer is on an old release and under maintenance you are obliged to help them work through the issue. If everyone was on the current release then not only would it reduce the burden on your helpdesk, it will also help stop your customers getting frustrated with the problem in the first place.
☐	6.1.20 Do you need to add new capability to your product?	This could either be the driver for a complete rewrite or a strategic approach to add new capability via Azure to enhance the existing on-premises offering.

Questions for suits > Why are we considering Azure?

☒	Question	Why this matters
☐	6.1.21 Are the varied target deployment setups at customers increasing your support costs?	You may define very clearly the operating environment for your software. However each customer will have their unique setup with subtle differences e.g. software versions, application of patches and service packs, network topology and speeds. This can create challenges to support when trying to troubleshoot a customer problem. This may mean having to invest in dedicated remote connectivity or even on site visits with the associated costs. Would it be easier if there was a single standardized deployment platform with someone else responsible for ensuring the patches etc were applied and tested?
☐	6.1.22 Do you need to make your solution more responsive to change?	One of the challenges with the traditional on-premises software model is that it typically works on an annual product lifecycle. This would be fine if your code had no bugs and your market sector did not change from one year to the next. However for many businesses this is not the case and whilst bugs can be addressed through service patches it may not be as simple to change business processes within a fast moving market sector. With the centrally managed nature of an Azure offering and the typically more frequent release cycle there is the option to deliver changes more rapidly and make these available to all customers.

Questions for suits > Why are we considering Azure?

☒	Question	Why this matters
☐	6.1.23 Can you shorten sales cycles?	There are a number of options to reduce the time to value for the customer and hence shorten the sales cycle: Removing the need to install your software at the client. Being able to demonstrate the production systems capability directly to the business line budget holder. Removing the need for the involvement of the IT department. The caveat should be added that, even though you can bypass the IT department it is probably a good idea long term to keep them on side.
☐	6.1.24 Will Azure's flexible charging models make it easier for customers to purchase?	If you can offer flexible payment terms e.g. monthly billing rather than a large upfront fee, then the budget holder may have authority to sign off the costs directly. Also being able to OPEX the costs with clear options to cease payment may reduce the concerns about lock in and budget constraints. However remember that for some businesses CAPEX is still their preferred budgeting approach, so make sure you can still accept upfront cash!
☐	6.1.25 Can you reduce barriers to entry for new customers, users or departments?	For new customers your mature product or pricing models may just be too complex for them. Maybe you can offer a version to provide a taste of the minimum functionality. You may consider offering this at a significantly reduced price (or even free). You can also look at free trial periods to get the user over the initial spend barriers.

Questions for suits > Why are we considering Azure?

☒	Question	Why this matters
☐	6.1.26 Can you improve time to market?	As with other items listed above Azure provides the opportunity to introduce new ideas and functionality to all customers at a much faster rate than the traditional on-premises model. Can you take advantage of this to bring new innovative ideas to market or to rapidly meet new legislative needs?
☐	6.1.27 Do you need to offer globalized reach with local presence?	Many of the current Cloud platforms will offer global reach, however this is provided from only a few locations, typically based in North America. Microsoft are investing in data centers so that Azure can be provisioned for customers from geo-local facilities. This can have hugely positive implications e.g. ability to support local legal requirements, local taxation regulations, political benefits of using local resources etc.

6.2 Is Azure right for my customers?

So you are happy that your motivations for looking at Azure as a Cloud delivery platform are sound. We now turn our focus on your customer.

As covered in the introductory chapters, Azure is a significant investment for Microsoft. Understandably there will be a lot of marketing noise extolling the benefits of Azure both to Microsoft partners and the industry in general. However if the capabilities that Azure offers do not align with the requirements and service needs of your customers then should you be going ahead?

It may be that you position yourself as driving thinking about the use of IT within your customers and therefore you must lead not follow. Even so, if you cannot articulate the mapping of their needs to Azure (even if they are not yet aware of this mapping) then you may have problems as you go forward.

You may be confident that Azure is the right technical approach for your customers. However, it may still not be appropriate due to other non-technical considerations. Being armed with these Smart Questions will help you identify customer concerns and either work with them to address the issues or recognise them as genuine show stoppers.

Questions for suits > Is Azure right for my customers?

☒	Question	Why this matters
☐	6.2.1 Are your customers in a bleeding edge sector?	Azure is new and this alone may create concerns with some customers. However, for companies who are used to being on the bleeding edge this concern is mitigated and they are less likely to be phased by the relative newness of the Cloud and specifically Azure.
☐	6.2.2 Are your customers conservative in nature?	Many companies have a conservative style and to a greater or lesser extent are risk averse. They will not want to lead, being more comfortable to wait for mainstream adoption and then follow. In this case trying to force a sale may be counterproductive and simply frustrate your valued customer. In this situation, it may be appropriate for you to establish a trusted advisor role and take the high ground saying you will watch this space and come back later. Alternatively, you could minimize the Cloud impact, by taking a more conservative approach, using Azure in a very specific or targeted way.
☐	6.2.3 Do your customers have an aversion to Microsoft?	For various reasons some business are not comfortable with Microsoft. They may use tools such as Office out of necessity/compatibility. But, outsourcing core business applications to a Microsoft owned and managed data center may be one step too far.
☐	6.2.4 Are your customers in a high growth sector?	Businesses that are growing fast whether through business success or acquisitions may require flexible access to infrastructure or rapid provisioning for new users. Azure based solutions could provide them with both flexibility and reduced investment costs.

Questions for suits > Is Azure right for my customers?

☒	**Question**	**Why this matters**
☐	6.2.5 Are your customers struggling or under pressure?	Obviously, you need to be careful about investing for customers who may not be around. However offering them a switch to OPEX charging may be exactly what they are looking for and may help them ride out any downturn. You will then be in "position one" to support them as things pick up.
☐	6.2.6 Do your customers have significant existing infrastructure investments e.g. data center?	The cost savings and other benefits of going to Azure may look great but if there is a huge accounting write off then this may not be financially acceptable. In addition, the politics of changing course after previous investments may be difficult for key stakeholders. Of course, there is the counter position where previous investments have failed and a new person has been given the job to make things better. You could be their best friend with a quick to deploy solution and no CAPEX.
☐	6.2.7 Have large investments been made in on-premises applications?	As with infrastructure investments, this can be a barrier to progress. Although again, if previous investments have failed then an Azure solution may be the perfect answer. However, it is also important to look at Azure as a complementary technology and an extension to existing technologies and investments. Could it be the icing on the cake, instead of a whole new cake?
☐	6.2.8 Is there a need for global anywhere, anytime access?	Provision of global access to systems has traditionally required large investments and typically been the domain of large enterprises. However the Cloud and in particular Azure with the global data center deployments makes this available even for the SME.

Questions for suits > Is Azure right for my customers?

☒	Question	Why this matters
☐	6.2.9 Is there a high peak load with low frequency of use capacity pattern?	Organizations have traditionally had to invest in infrastructure that meets their peak load requirements even if these peak loads are infrequent, leading to low overall utilization. This has in turn excluded many businesses that could valuably use a solution but have not been able to justify the high average cost per use. The "pay as you use" and flexible pricing models offered by Azure can fundamentally change the price point for these solution types and open the offering to a completely new group of customers.
☐	6.2.10 Are there specific seasonal usage patterns with low or no utilization between?	A more extreme case of 6.2.9 is where the use of the system is focused on specific events. Examples could be sporting events such as the Olympics or Wimbledon or a retail store's annual sale. In these cases, there is a huge resource requirement for a few weeks and then back to almost zero. Using Azure would mean only paying for the infrastructure needed to meet the demand and only for the period required.
☐	6.2.11 Do your customers have significant scaling requirements?	Where organizations see significant growth in resource requirement they typically have to either a) build out infrastructure to their most optimistic projections (which could still be wrong if things take off) or b) build out the minimum and hope they can scale quick enough if things go well. In either scenario there are also investment steps where an additional "batch" of kit is purchased. The flexible scaling arrangement available with Azure means that you can offer exactly what the customer needs, no more and no less. If their needs vary then the resources can flex both up and down. This in turn offers you lots of commercial options (see later).

51

Questions for suits > Is Azure right for my customers?

☒	Question	Why this matters
☐	6.2.12 Are customers looking to reduce internal IT headcount?	For many companies the costs of maintaining the correct skills and staff coverage required to run their own infrastructure is becoming draining. This is especially true where this is a non core aspect to their business. Utilizing the economies of an outsourced, shared resource, Azure infrastructure and thus freeing up budgets for core activities could be very attractive.
☐	6.2.13 Are your customers looking to avoid upcoming infrastructure investments?	At various times infrastructure needs to be refreshed. This may be to replace inefficient/old hardware, to provide greater storage or because of the demands of new software e.g. requiring 64bit hardware. If your Azure based offering can link into this cycle then there is a potentially significant investment avoidance saving to include in your benefits model.
☐	6.2.14 Does the customer have workloads that startup and then are shut down?	Companies may have workloads that require resources for a short period and are then closed down e.g. project based activities, R&D etc. If there is spare capacity in the existing infrastructure then great. But what happens if this requires new CAPEX spend? Would the ability to add resources and users on demand and only pay for the period of "up time" on an OPEX basis make previously uneconomic projects now justifiable?
☐	6.2.15 Is the customer looking for Blue Ocean[19] opportunities?	The fundamental changes in the delivery and commercial models associated with the Cloud in general and specifically Azure may open up opportunities for customers to change their market positioning – to change the game

---

[19] *Blue Ocean Strategy* by W. Chan Kim & Renee Mauborgne

Questions for suits > Is Azure right for my customers?

☒	Question	Why this matters
☐	6.2.16 Does the client need to differentiate themselves in a Red Ocean (see Blue Ocean)?	Where price is the key market share determinant, the commercial models available with Azure may offer smart differentiation for your customers and in turn new opportunities for you.
☐	6.2.17 Is the customer looking to roll out standardized processes globally?	Trying to co-ordinate the deployment of a standardized process across a global organization (large or small) can be challenging on many levels. Using on-premises software can add to this, even from a simple roll out perspective. An Azure solution with its centralized deployment options and ability to scale may remove some of these challenges, and Azures localized data center capability could be a key differentiator.
☐	6.2.18 Does your customer have a wider program of change that Azure can be part of?	Is there is a wider agenda for change, outsourcing etc that your Azure offering is consistent with? If so then this could reduce sales barriers and make your offering more attractive.
☐	6.2.19 Do your customers have a Green Agenda?	There is a lot of focus on Green issues at the moment. Depending on what you read data centers are seen as good (they have higher utilization levels) or bad (the simple measure of energy consumption). Irrespective of where you start, Azure with its Generation 4 data centers is a highly efficient Cloud platform (Power Usage Effectiveness [PUE] of 1.22). If your customers have a question about "green credentials" in their commercial enquiries then Azure should allow you to offer a positive response.

Questions for suits > Is Azure right for my customers?

☒	Question	Why this matters
☐	6.2.20 What are the customer's requirements for data migration?	If a customer is replacing an existing system then it is likely that they will have data that needs to be migrated. Even in a new system there may be seed data that is required to configure the system before it can be used. This data may exist in multiple places. Does the data need to be cleansed, aggregated or de-duplicated? How will the data migration process be validated, especially if there have been significant changes to the data during migration? These are all potential blockers to adoption OR could be a professional services opportunity.
☐	6.2.21 Is there a large quantity of data that needs to be migrated into Windows Azure at the outset?	Depending on the quantities involved, the physical time taken for the process of data import and validation may be material to the overall project plan.
☐	6.2.22 Do the staff being targeted to use the service have the correct capabilities?	By changing the commercials, delivery models etc there may be groups of users who it is now economical to provide systems to. Have they previously been exposed to IT systems as part of their job. Will they have the required skills to use these systems, will they require training?
☐	6.2.23 Will there be a significant staff training requirement?	Any new system will mean change. The current users may be more than capable of acquiring the new skills, however they will probably need time to familiarize themselves. This may be possible in an informal manner, or it could require formal training sessions. How much disruption will this cause and what budget needs to be allocated?

Questions for suits > Is Azure right for my customers?

☒	Question	Why this matters
☐	6.2.24 Is there a need for distinct segregation of infrastructure?	For some systems the risk profiling by the customer requires that the systems are deployed on infrastructure that can be demonstrated as physically segregated. You should consider whether Azure provides the segregation required.
☐	6.2.25 Are the customers financial models suited for evaluating Cloud offerings?	Are the customers' ROI calculators designed for a more traditional on-premises sales model? Is there an assumption that there will be a large CAPEX investment up front with lower ongoing charges or cash flow based on fixed annual upfront fees rather than monthly variable ones? This can make Cloud projects with annuity revenue models appear less attractive. Also remember that for some customers CAPEX is good. You could create your own ROI/TCO tool. Or consider using ones provided by Microsoft.
☐	6.2.26 Is the customer subject to specific infrastructure requirements?	In certain situations customers are subject to clearly defined infrastructure requirements. This could be a result of their own risk review, external legislative requirements or requirements from their downstream customers. For example the UK government assesses the risk profile of information systems and assigns them a code such as IL2, IL3 etc. At IL4 (and depending on the assessor IL3) you are only supposed to use hardware from an "approved" list. Azure does not provide the flexibility of a customized data center facility. If Azure does not meet the customer's requirements then you are unlikely to get Microsoft to make changes.

Questions for suits > Is Azure right for my customers?

☒	Question	Why this matters
☐	6.2.27 Do your customers have specific in-country data requirements?	Although Azure offers data centers that are geo-located it may be that even this is not enough and there may be a requirement for specific in-country data center facilities. Even where there is a data center in your country, if there are multiple data centers in your geographic region then your data could be in any of these.
☐	6.2.28 What are the requirements for data destruction?	The design of Azure means that data is stored in multiple locations to ensure recovery in the event of physical hardware failure. For many customers this is a key benefit. However this lack of certainty of the physical location of all copies of the data could be an issue for customers who have specific requirements for data destruction.
☐	6.2.29 What are your customers audit requirements?	Audit is a wide ranging subject, from data center management all the way to recording individual actions by system users. You need to be clear about what requirements exist with the customer. This will allow you to determine if this is a basic manual process, something provided by Microsoft's data center reporting, information provided by Azure or something you will need to provide custom code for within your application.
☐	6.2.30 Has the customer quantified the organizational change costs?	There may be significant savings or benefits by moving to Azure. However if the cost to achieve these savings either in hard cash, morale, good will etc are not in line with these benefits then the project could easily stall. If part of the benefits are based on organizational savings e.g. headcount reductions then the costs of achieving these savings need to be considered.

Questions for suits > Is Azure right for my customers?

☒	Question	Why this matters
☐	6.2.31 Are there significant investments required to achieve the Cloud benefits?	If employees are now going to access their day to day applications via the internet, will there need to be an increase in bandwidth? Will contracts need to be renegotiated? If new users are going to be given access to the "low cost" service will they need to be provided with a computer?
☐	6.2.32 Do write offs of existing investments need to be taken into account?	So you have a fantastic low cost Azure offering with improved functionality. However last year the client invested USD 2m in hardware and software with a 5 year write off. What will the CFO say when he is asked to write off USD1.6m?
☐	6.2.33 What data retention policies are required?	Some customers may have regulatory requirements to keep copies of data for extended periods. Can you meet these requirements with Azure?
☐	6.2.34 Can Azure meet the required SLAs?	Service Level Agreements should be central to any service and are worthy of a book in their own right. However customers are particularly sensitive when it comes to external services. You should be careful that the client is being reasonable and they are making a fair comparison to their existing SLAs when stipulating SLAs for your Azure based offering. Do their current systems offer 99.9% uptime, including a service credit if this is not met?
☐	6.2.35 Does the customer have downstream contracts with specific requirements?	The services offered by Azure are largely fixed. If there are specific clauses that require flexibility that is not natively on offer in Azure then it may either be impossible or cost prohibitive to deliver.

Questions for suits > Is Azure right for my customers?

☒	Question	Why this matters
☐	6.2.36 Does the customer operate across multiple legal jurisdictions?	Although one of the opportunities for the Cloud is to deliver solutions on a global basis, this brings with it challenges especially in the area of legal jurisdiction. One of the benefits of Azure over a number of other Cloud platforms is that Microsoft have invested (and are continuing to invest) in data centers in different geographies.
☐	6.2.37 Does the customer require specific security clearance for Azure data center staff?	Although all data centers will pride themselves on the quality of their staff this does not mean that it will be possible to ensure they meet a clients specific requirements for security clearance.
☐	6.2.38 Will the customer want to replicate the Azure infrastructure in an alternative location as part of their Disaster Recovery planning?	Although there will be alternative ways of hosting the applications that have been delivered on Azure, the actual Azure platform is only available in Microsoft data centers.
☐	6.2.39 What are the customers backup and DR requirements?	Microsoft has put a lot of effort into delivering a robust platform that offers high levels of resilience. However, Azure is also a largely fixed service. If clients have specific DR requirements and these are not covered by Azure then it may be costly (or impossible) to deliver them. However, as with SLAs make sure the client is being realistic. It is likely that for many customers the levels of resilience provided by the Azure platform are far in excess of their current situation.

Questions for suits > Is Azure right for my customers?

☒	Question	Why this matters
☐	6.2.40 Does the customer require physical access to the data centers?	Some clients may wish to be present at DR events or to physically inspect the hardware that their applications or data is located on. All well managed data centers have very strict rules about external access. However, the shared nature of the Azure environment will make this even more restrictive.

6.3 Is Azure right for my business?

Our motivations are sound, Azure can meet the service needs of our customers, so full steam ahead. STOP.

Despite all the desire and opportunity on offer, moving to the Cloud and using Azure as your tool of choice will have potentially significant impacts upon your business. Finance, billing, development lifecycles, sales and marketing, in fact your whole business may be affected.

Without a clear understanding of these impacts you cannot assess the risks – it would be like jumping off the edge not knowing if it was a small step or the edge of a cliff.

Azure has the potential to be a fundamental game changing technology within the IT industry, however there are risks and to be one of the winners you need to manage these risks. This means understanding them. Even if you are using the Cloud and Azure as part of a last roll of the dice to save the business don't further increase the risks for the sake of a little planning.

Note: The commercial considerations are such a key topic that these are discussed within their own section.

Questions for suits > Is Azure right for my business?

☒	Question	Why this matters
☐	6.3.1 Is the management team fully supportive?	Any change within a business can bring challenges and this will need the management team to be supportive of each other to increase the chances of success. Depending on the choices you make the Cloud has the potential to be highly disruptive. Of course this does not mean the management team should simply follow like sheep as there will almost certainly be value in rigorous discussion of the possible options.
☐	6.3.2 Have you gained the support of key influencers amongst your employees?	Change is a funny thing and people react differently. Within your business there are likely to be key influencers who can influence the rest of the staff. Their influence is often not linked to the position in the organizational hierarchy. However a little effort up front can reap huge rewards as you progress.
☐	6.3.3 Are your investors fully informed and supportive?	A move to the Cloud is likely to require additional investment and the revenue model used to cover this investment may be different from your current one (e.g. license to annuity). Your investors may be highly supportive or they could raise concerns. Although asking for forgiveness afterwards may seem easier than gaining approval in advance this could be a high risk strategy.

Questions for suits > Is Azure right for my business?

☒	**Question**	**Why this matters**
☐	6.3.4 Are your planning cycles consistent with using Azure?	The annual release cycle for traditional software has been a strong driver of business planning. Marketing, development, sales etc. are geared up for the big annual launch. Do your planning cycles need to change to reflect more frequent software updates or fluctuating capacity utilization by customers that impacts monthly cash flow. Will this require a change in the frequency of board/management/sales meetings?
☐	6.3.5 Are your staff ready for change?	You may have the correct capabilities within your company, but not everyone is comfortable with change. Some people may suddenly shine, whilst other previously strong staff members may fade or worse become blockers. Recognizing this and effectively managing the change process will be a key aspect of a successful move to Azure.
☐	6.3.6 Is your business comfortable relying on Microsoft?	Being in a situation where a 3rd party directly impacts your ability to control the service you offer to your customer can be uncomfortable. With on-premises software it is normally the customer's responsibility to provide and manage the infrastructure. If it goes wrong then you come in as the knight in shining armor to save the day. Now you are responsible for the end to end service as far as the customer is concerned. But in reality you are dependent upon Microsoft to meet their Azure SLAs promises.

Questions for suits > Is Azure right for my business?

☒	Question	Why this matters
☐	6.3.7 Can you leverage Microsoft's marketing investments in Azure?	Microsoft is making a big bet on Azure. With that bet comes a large marketing budget. By engaging with Microsoft through your partner manager about your experiences with Azure you may be part of a case study, or invited to speak at events. You need to make a conscious decision to do this, it takes real effort and you may not be the only one. However if this fits within your marketing plans then there are real opportunities for exposure.
☐	6.3.8 How will the development costs of delivering on Azure be funded?	There will be costs to develop and deploy applications on Azure. Depending on your choices these costs will vary. It may be that the costs can be covered through your existing R&D budgets or you may choose to seek additional external funding. Whatever your decision, being clear up front will be a key aspect of your risk management process.
☐	6.3.9 Do you have existing investments that will need to be written off?	Start-ups have the advantage that they have no legacy investments to consider. However, most companies do not have this luxury and need to consider what the consequences of change will be. Are there existing software or hardware investments that will need to be written off and will these change the economics. Clearly these cannot be ignored, however there is a risk that they create so much inertia that the right decisions are not made. (assuming of course that Azure is the right decision)
☐	6.3.10 Is the business experienced with managing partners?	Apart from Microsoft it is likely that you will have additional partnerships. The effective management of these will be important and can be a key factor in your marketplace differentiation and success.

Questions for suits > Is Azure right for my business?

☒	Question	Why this matters
☐	6.3.11 Is this an opportunity to cancel or renegotiate contracts with suppliers?	Moving your deployment platform to Azure could be a great opportunity to review costs within the business that just exist because they always have. If you are reducing the number of servers you run can the support agreements be re-negotiated or even cancelled? If you are going to expand another area of the business as part of your move to Azure does this allow you to get better volume discounts or to engage with a partner who offers better value?
☐	6.3.12 Do you have the correct technical skills?	Will there be new skills required? Will this require training or hiring new staff? Have you budgeted for this in your funding plans?
☐	6.3.13 Do you have the correct sales and marketing skills?	There are established sales and marketing approaches for traditional software. These are often based around face to face interaction. With a wider audience that is often self educated this dynamic has the potential to be significantly changed. The new medium of social media may now compliment or even replace your existing models. Your top salesperson may suddenly feel like a fish out of water. A young enthusiastic member of your marketing team may suddenly shine.
☐	6.3.14 What provision for local professional services will you require?	With global reach comes both opportunity and challenges. The idea that once in the Cloud all on-premises requirements are gone is a misnomer. Integration, training configuration etc are great revenue opportunities. Do you already have a global services operation that can be utilized? Do you want to set one up? Or do you want to partner with local providers to allow for rapid scale even if this means sharing revenue?

☒	Question	Why this matters
☐	6.3.15 Will you need to provide local support across multiple geographies?	One of the benefits of Azure is the ability to provide global reach on effectively unlimited scale. If this means entering new overseas markets how will you handle support in the local timezone? Will you need a 24 hour call center? Who will physically go on site if required? If you cannot offer this it may be a blocker to sales.
☐	6.3.16 Are there infrastructure investments you need to make?	An external data center is now an integral part of your development and deployment infrastructure. Will this mean greater bandwidth across your internet connection requiring a higher speed connection? What backup facilities do you have in place to ensure that connectivity is maintained? Will developers require new machines to support the IDE and the local instance of the Azure environment? Do you need to upgrade software e.g. to latest version of Visual Studio (even if you get this free as part of your Microsoft Partner Network/MSDN membership there maybe deployment costs)
☐	6.3.17 Can you utilize your existing developer skills?	If you are already using Visual Studio and any .NET language then you are an obvious candidate to benefit from the efforts Microsoft have made to ensure that Azure fits into your existing developer experience. However Microsoft have gone to considerable lengths to open Azure up to other languages e.g. PHP and this is likely to continue. (See questions in Chapter 7).

Questions for suits > Is Azure right for my business?

☒	Question	Why this matters
☐	6.3.18 Do you present yourself as a Green business?	Is being green a part of your marketing differentiation? If so then Azure has a good story to tell. The efficiency that Microsoft have been able to achieve with their Generation 4 Data center model is significantly better than traditional data centers (Power Usage Effectiveness of 1.22 and improving). This efficiency story could be a good fit with your marketing message.

6.4 Commercial considerations

One could easily argue that we have, as the saying goes, left the best until last. The different commercial options that Cloud Computing makes possible are without doubt one of the most significant changes from the traditional on-premise world. Therefore understanding these changes in the context of Azure is critical. If all of the hype around the Cloud is to be believed then this is actually simple:

<!Start Dream Sequence!>

1. You develop a brand new application
2. Deploy it to Azure and make it available globally
3. Initially this is a free "beta" offer
4. Having put out regular tweets on Twitter you build up a huge user base
5. With frequent (monthly) updates you enhance the capability
6. You are approached by a Silicon Valley investor who offers you $20m for 1% of the business valuing you at $2Bn
7. You decide it is time to work out how to monetize this fantastic user base
8. And that's where it all started to get tricky......

<!Wake from Dream Sequence with large dose of reality!>

Of course the real world is not like this and there are many commercial areas to consider. Just because you can offer monthly billing is that right for you or your customer, are there other options? What about you existing product pricing?

In many ways the models for commercialization of the Cloud have been framed in a way that is friendly to start ups and potentially challenging or even threatening to established companies. Does this mean that all established businesses must throw everything away and reinvent themselves? Or can they look at the new options and consider how these can be best utilized within their existing business? For some there will be a revolution and for

Questions for suits > Commercial considerations

others an evolutionary approach will be the right way. The real point is that there are choices.

This section cannot cover the whole subject area of commercials. However, we trust that even where we have missed something that is relevant to you, the process of reviewing these questions will help you generate your own areas to consider. Even with this caveat there are a lot of questions and these are ordered in the following general areas:

- About your offering and route to market
- Cost considerations
- Pricing and Sales
- Supporting process factors

NB The questions relating to legal areas towards the end of this section should not be considered legal advice. We offer these questions as a guide to things you may wish to consider and if you do decide to seek legal advice they may speed up the process and save you some money!

Questions for suits > Commercial considerations

☒	Question	Why this matters
☐	6.4.1 Are you considering a global offering for your product?	If you already have global distribution then you will have had to consider issues such as differential pricing, exchange rate conversions, invoicing in multiple currencies, contract terms being localized etc. If your move to Azure is to create global reach for your offering for the first time then these may need careful consideration.
☐	6.4.2 Do you know the buying culture of your target customers?	If you are offering a solution to your existing customers then the answer is hopefully yes. However if you are entering new markets then things may be different. Web centric buyers are motivated differently. If you are now targeting a different demographic then are they motivated by the same factors as your existing customers?
☐	6.4.3 Are you using a channel route to market?	Using a channel route can offer many benefits e.g. credibility if you are entering a new area, scale without having direct headcount. However it can also create challenges. If you have an existing channel do they have the correct skills? Will there be conflict with existing channel partners if you appoint new ones?
☐	6.4.4 Will you have a direct sales channel?	Do your current sales team have the correct skills? How will you avoid channel conflict if you are also use a channel route to market? These are not new issues, however your move to Azure may make them new for you.

Questions for suits > Commercial considerations

☒	Question	Why this matters
☐	6.4.5 What impact will an Azure offering have on your existing products?	If the Azure offering provides incremental sales to existing customers or opens up new markets then great. But what happens if it simply steals from your existing customer base? There is the potential for reductions in revenue. Existing customers may feel like they are being over charged and want to move. You may have little choice but beware of product cannibalism.
☐	6.4.6 Does your offering have to pay its own way?	There are a number of further questions in this area, however it is a basic starting point that can affect many of your commercial decisions. Do the sales of this offering have to cover all of the costs and make a profit?
☐	6.4.7 Is the offering a lead into other revenue streams?	Are there downstream revenue opportunities that will be influenced by this offering? Can you subsidize the costs of this offering from these downstream revenues? It could be a simple "let me show you how good we are" application that you offer for free as part of your marketing. Or it could be part of a model where you initially offer a low cost/free Lite version and then upsell to a charged for, Professional version. The key is to be clear that this is your approach and know where you expect the influenced revenues to come from so you can measure the success and hence justify the costs.
☐	6.4.8 Is your Azure offering an add-on to existing products?	A move to Azure does not have to be a revolutionary leap with a brand new product. There may be great ways to enhance the functionality of or reduce the operating costs of an existing on-premises offering. How will you charge for this? As part of your normal license/maintenance, or a separate monthly fee (fixed or variable).

Questions for suits > Commercial considerations

☒	Question	Why this matters
☐	6.4.9 Which of Microsoft's Azure pricing models is right for you and your customers?	Pricing for Azure will evolve over time and options may come and others go. At the time of writing there are 3 broad areas. Pay as you go, Commitment pricing and pricing linked to Volume license agreements. Does a truly flexible pay as you go model allow you to match prices exactly to consumption and drive differentiation? If you can predict loads and make forward commitment to Microsoft, will the discounts under Commitment pricing change your price point? Can you be smart and use a customer's Azure usage rights against their existing volume licenses? This area will change and it is important that you keep watching this space.
☐	6.4.10 How do the costs for Azure compare to your existing platform?	Having a clear before/after comparison on costs is a key element in justifying a move to Azure. You may have existing costs models that can be updated with the Azure pricing. Or you may wish to utilize TCO tools that Microsoft supply. Getting this right could help highlight areas that benefit more from Azure than anticipated or make it clear that Azure is not right in this instance. Azure may provide you with many benefits beyond your current offering and this may make comparing old with new difficult. However this is still a valuable exercise.

Questions for suits > Commercial considerations

☒	Question	Why this matters
☐	6.4.11 How do Azure prices compare to competing platforms?	Microsoft is not the only provider of Cloud infrastructure or platforms. Knowing how the other providers' prices compare is important. Be careful however when you make this comparison to compare like for like. The different providers offer different things. Some are PaaS and others IaaS. Be clear what your specific usage scenarios require and don't rely of generic use cases. There is no point paying a premium for services you do not need. Equally however it can be a false economy to provide your own framework and platform management in order to save a few dollars in monthly charges
☐	6.4.12 What is the nature of your offering and how does this link to Azure pricing?	The costs for using Azure vary based on a number of factors e.g. the services you use, the data volumes you consume and the bandwidth you utilize. It is key to understand how your application operates in relation to these charges. It may be that the economics for your particular offering are marginal and therefore the costs of migration cannot be justified. By considering this at design time (See questions in Chapter 7) it might be possible to be more efficient in a particular area and change the cost profile.

Questions for suits > Commercial considerations

☒	Question	Why this matters
☐	6.4.13 How do you manage the costs of scaling resource utilization to meet user demand?	One of the big benefits of Azure is that you can scale the resources used to almost unlimited levels. This is great if your pricing models allow you to fully recover these increased costs. However uncontrolled scaling could lead to some big mismatches between costs and income. Should you offer different scaling depending on whether a customer is on Professional fully flexible charge plan OR a Lite fixed price offering. Do you stay fully in control of cost by manually monitoring utilization (people cost overhead) or try and automate some of the processes?
☐	6.4.14 How do you manage different billing periods from Suppliers?	Using Azure will mean billing from Microsoft in some form. But you may also be using other suppliers services to deliver the overall offering to the customer. It is unlikely that the billing from these differing suppliers will be consistent (periods, advance/arrears/fixed variable etc). How will you "hide" this complexity from your customer without leaving yourself exposed?
☐	6.4.15 Will you need additional Azure environments that are not directly paid for by the customer?	There is more discussion on this in Chapter 7. However your costs of delivering the solution to the customer may need to include separate "non production" environments e.g. UAT, system test, Demo. How will the costs for these be factored into your pricing?
☐	6.4.16 Does the end user pay directly for your offering?	It may seem old fashioned in the new world of the Cloud but it helps a business if someone actually pays for the services they offer! The boring but well proven model for this is to actually get the user to pay directly.

Questions for suits > Commercial considerations

☒	Question	Why this matters
☐	6.4.17 Will a Freemium model work for you?	The model where a small number of users who get high value from a service actually pay and this allows the others to have truly free access to the service is highly topical[20]. However is does require sufficient users of the system to create a large enough area of the value curve where people are paying.
☐	6.4.18 Is there enough value for a sponsor to cover the costs for their ecosystem?	Company A would like all of their suppliers to use a service because of the huge back office savings they can make. They may be willing to sponsor the service so that it can be offered free to all of their suppliers. The cost model is likely to generate less revenue than the theoretical revenue if every supplier could be charged. However you massively reduce the cost of sales, payment collection costs etc and you have mitigated the variable of user uptake.
☐	6.4.19 Is there enough user volume to consider ad-funding?	Google have demonstrated that there is a lot of money to be made with ads. However the volumes of user "eyeballs" to make ad-funding realistic are very large. It may be right for you, but make sure you do your sums first.
☐	6.4.20 Do you charge on an Annuity basis?	Annuity pricing is seen by many as the only model in a Cloud world. Many suppliers including Microsoft have linked their pricing to a periodic annuity charge. There are many benefits to this model and it could well be the right one for you. But it is not the only choice.

---

[20] Chris Anderson "Free: The Future of a Radical Price"

Questions for suits > Commercial considerations

☒	Question	Why this matters
☐	6.4.21 Do you consider the offering as JAM (just another module)?	Are you extending an existing on-premises application with an Azure based module? You could charge for this new module on an Annuity basis (e.g. the Microsoft Payroll module for their Small Business Accounting). Or you could make it part of your standard licensing fee. The usage may be sufficiently stable to allow for the fixed charges that this implies. It could be that the savings you make in other areas by moving this module to the Cloud justify any variation in costs vs new charges.
☐	6.4.22 Do you charge one off setup fees?	Just because you are now delivering from Azure does not mean that all setup costs have disappeared. Depending on the complexity and the degree to which the user can self service the costs you bare will vary. These costs could be included in the service fee or you may decide to separate them out as one off setup fees. Areas such as data migration and cleansing or system configuration could be considered.
☐	6.4.23 Are there follow up professional fees?	There could be a great professional services opportunity either directly by you, or for 3rd party partners. Customers are often thinking about the Cloud in the context of a wider change program. There may be revenue opportunities if you look. E.g. Training, business process improvement, support services etc.

Questions for suits > Commercial considerations

☒	Question	Why this matters
☐	6.4.24 Do you offer try before you buy?	Many Cloud services offer a try before you buy option. The logic is that with the less connected sales process you have not had "sales time" with the customer to show them the benefits. By offering them a free trial they learn to like the offering and then convert. The key is to get the conversion. Areas to consider are how long is the trial (longer periods do NOT increase conversion). Can you link your trial period to similar offers from you delivery partners e.g. Microsoft. How do you ensure that the customer uses the service during the trial (reduce the time to value). How do you make the conversion at the end of the trial so easy they just do it?
☐	6.4.25 Do you charge in advance or arrears?	In advance has the attraction that you have cash in the bank and if the customer does not pay then you turn off their access to the service. However if you are running a pay-as-you-go pricing model then you do not know until after the charge period what the consumption was. Having a pay in advance with a retrospective adjustment for actual use could get complex. Although that is how many utility companies work their monthly payment models i.e. a fixed price every period and then after a confirmed meter reading the period price is adjusted up or down. Lots of options…

Questions for suits > Commercial considerations

☒	Question	Why this matters
☐	6.4.26 How dynamically do you allow a customer to add or remove resources?	Azure makes it easy for you to increase or decrease the resources you consume and hence the payments you make to Microsoft. However, this may not be the right approach for your pricing to your customers. Do you allow addition and removal of users at will or do you have some period of lock in? If you are covering setup costs within your fees then there will be a minimum period to recover these e.g. Mobile phone companies have well established lock-in plans to recover their investments in you as a customer.
☐	6.4.27 Do you have a variable or fixed pricing model?	Variable may be the flavor of the day, but it does not have to be the only approach. Clients may actually prefer a known fixed cost even if this is a little more expensive. You could band users into high/medium/low usage and charge accordingly. You could have a small fixed charge with a variable top up component.
☐	6.4.28 Do you offer a consumption or user pricing model?	These two approaches have their pros and cons. Consumption allows you to match your incoming costs with your charges (plus markup). However, there can be complexities in measuring, capturing and allocating the consumption costs from multiple suppliers across multiple users. The user pricing model simplifies this. However, you are potentially exposed if you get your user charging/banding wrong and costs exceed charging.

77

Questions for suits > Commercial considerations

☒	Question	Why this matters
☐	6.4.29 How often do you invoice?	Monthly billing often appears to be the norm. However, even where the stated charges are monthly the reality can be that you actually pay quarterly or even annually. This is true for some of the very well known Cloud companies such as Salesforce. If you already carry out monthly invoicing then great. However if you are moving from large annual bills to your 150 existing customers to low value monthly billing for 25,000 customers, then be prepared for a process shock.
☐	6.4.30 How will you measure an individual company or users consumption?	Microsoft will offer a detailed breakdown of the Azure services consumed and their associated costs. However, this will be at the services level and Microsoft will not be able to know which of your users consumed these resources. Your ability to measure/record the individual users consumption may affect how you end up pricing. (See questions in Chapter 7).
☐	6.4.31 Do you offer Service Credits?	Microsoft will provide you with service credits if Azure does not meet the stated SLAs. Do you offer service credits to your customers? If so how much and on what basis? The delivery of the offering is likely to depend upon factors other than just Azure, how do you factor these other areas into your service credits?
☐	6.4.32 Can your internal processes scale to meet demand?	If you are now selling to thousands of customers on a global basis, can your internal processes and systems scale with this. Cash collection, bad debt management, multi-currency accounting systems, volume based microbilling, accepting credit card payments etc.

Questions for suits > Commercial considerations

☒	Question	Why this matters
☐	6.4.33 How sensitive is your pricing to external factors?	It is normal for most if not all of the key cost components of an on-premises offering to be under the complete control of the supplier. With a Cloud offering there are now key factors out of your control e.g. Azure pricing, 3rd party services for local support around the world, customer usage profiles. If your pricing models have poor assumptions related to these external factors then you can easily find yourself delivering your service at a loss. Do you need a "right to change clause"? Should you try and negotiate to only pay 3rd parties when you are paid?
☐	6.4.34 Will your sales compensation model have to change?	With license fees in advance it was easy to commission the salesperson. However, with monthly annuity this model either has to change or the company pays the salesperson and then takes a risk that the customer will stay and pay for the full term. This is a whole area for discussion in its own right and has the potential to be highly disruptive. However depending upon your choices (annual charges in advance) it may be much less of an issue than feared.
☐	6.4.35 Where do the contractual relationships lay?	Customers are probably going to want a single point of contract. You are probably going to want to own the relationship and hence be that single contractual point. However to deliver this you will have to consider the various parties involved with delivering the final offering. Can you back to back the commitments you make to your customer with your 3rd party partners e.g. SLAs. What is the exposure if you cannot back to back any terms?

Questions for suits > Commercial considerations

☒	Question	Why this matters
☐	6.4.36 Are there existing contractual terms that you are bound by?	Do existing contracts with either customers or suppliers need to be re-negotiated to reflect any changes that occur with a move to Azure? Can you offer better terms to a customer? Can you cancel 3rd party contracts and if so are there penalty clauses or lock-in periods? All of these could make a move to Azure more or less attractive.

Chapter 7

Questions for jeans

If you want creative workers, give them enough time to play.
John Cleese (English Actor/Comedian, 1939 -)

MOVING to Azure is a serious design decision. There are pros and cons. There are areas that have the potential to greatly simplify things. There are others that could add significant complexity.

In this chapter we explore the questions that would be of interest to the more technically minded within your business. To be very clear though, this is NOT a technical how-to guide.

In the introduction to the previous chapter, we suggested that it would be a good idea for the "suits" to read the technical questions. This would provide them with an insight to the technical delivery constraints and open their eyes to possibilities.

We now suggest to the "jeans" that you should read the business questions. Understanding the context and reasoning behind certain business decisions can be a great motivator.

7.1 The big picture

At the simplest level using Azure means running your application on servers owned and managed by Microsoft. This section contains those big picture questions that you need to ask upfront.

The first few questions in this section address what types of application might be best suited to Azure and encourage you to compare your application against these scenarios. This is followed by questions that address moving to Azure and the options to consider.

The heart of this section raises key questions about Azure. What level of service availability will you get? What performance can you expect? What are the scalability options for your application? How secure is Azure?

Finally, there are questions on future proofing your application. Perhaps you want to ease migration to Azure at a later time or have an exit strategy if Azure is not for you.

Questions for jeans > The big picture

☒	**Question**	**Why this matters**
☐	7.1.1 Where are you in the application lifecycle?	You may potentially encounter different challenges depending on where you are in the application lifecycle. Building a Greenfield application allows you to fully embrace the Azure architecture. Migrating a system to Azure may present issues as well as offer resolutions to problems such as integration and compatibility. Azure also offers the flexibility to create proof of concepts or value added services quickly and to deploy these at low cost. Consider whether to start with one or all of these strategies.
☐	7.1.2 What type of application are you creating (mission critical, value add service, internal, back office, reporting)?	Depending on what kind of application you are writing, Azure may be more or less compelling. Consider the importance of the application to your business and the cost of running this application. It may be more difficult to get executive sponsorship for moving a mission critical application than a value-add service. If you have a web application, computationally intensive solutions or analytical processing tools Azure is going to be far more compelling.[21] You need to carefully consider whether Azure is appropriate for your application.

---

[21] "Patterns For High Availability, Scalability, And Computing Power With Windows Azure" *http://msdn.microsoft.com/en-us/magazine/dd727504.aspx*

Questions for jeans > The big picture

☒	Question	Why this matters
☐	7.1.3 Do you need to integrate with other existing or 3rd party systems?	Integrating systems can be a big challenge. Azure provides support for this. This includes the ability to connect on-premises applications to Azure, along with providing interoperability with different identity provides for federated identity management. Consider your current integration challenges and whether the .NET Service Bus could simplify these. Consider your need for a centralized user access management system and whether the .NET Access Control Service could provide this.
☐	7.1.4 What type of database application are you creating?	SQL Azure provides a Cloud-based relational database built on SQL Server technology. SQL Azure itself provides scale, high availability and data protection. There are, however, some limitations including a restriction on the size of any individual database. Consider your needs and how these match against the capabilities of SQL Azure. Remember that whilst Azure offers the potential for huge scale the bigger you go the more you will have to think about your design.
☐	7.1.5 What strategies are there when moving to Azure? Is it all or nothing?	Azure is a group of services that interoperate well with each other. One advantage to moving all your systems to Azure is that there is one environment to understand and use. However, Azure is also designed to interoperate well with existing on-premises systems. Using just one part of Azure is also a reasonable option.

Questions for jeans > The big picture

☒	**Question**	**Why this matters**
☐	7.1.6 So, if you can mix and match on-premises and Azure services, what are my options?	There are a number of high-level scenarios that have been highlighted for ISVs[22], which could be generally applicable. Azure could be used for storage and to provide access to this data from an on-premises system. You could perform some or all of your processing on Azure. You might create a SaaS version of your system. You could combine an Azure hosted application with your on-premises system. The mix and match model will allow many more options.
☐	7.1.7 What types of application might migrate well to Azure?	Consider the architecture of Azure – does your system use a similar architecture today? Azure is based on a service oriented architecture. Systems with this type of architecture or a loosely coupled application architecture might migrate well. Azure also favors stateless applications and this should be considered when you look at your current applications.
☐	7.1.8 The application is certified for Windows Server. Will this make migration easier?	Applications certified for Windows Server will not run on Windows Azure unless they are ported[23].

---

[22] "Windows Azure and ISVs – A Guide for Decision Makers" *http://go.microsoft.com/fwlink/?LinkID=157857*

[23] *http://www.microsoft.com/azure/faq.mspx*

Questions for jeans > The big picture

☒	Question	Why this matters
☐	7.1.9 How do you move existing data to Azure?	Neither Windows Azure storage nor SQL Azure provides any specific features for bulk loading or moving data. It is not possible to provide a tape or have a disk mounted within the Azure data center. SSIS or the SQLCMD utility to bulk copy data may provide a reasonable mechanism to move data into SQL Azure. Consider the amount and the complexity of the data you need to move. Consider whether this is a one-off move or an ongoing requirement.
☐	7.1.10 What type of support will be provided for Azure?	Microsoft will offer a range of support options directly. Microsoft will also offer support through its partner ecosystem. The type of support for partners will depend on their certification. This includes business critical phone support.[24]
☐	7.1.11 What level of service availability does your application require?	This is likely to be related to the type of system that you are considering for Azure. Azure has different charges and SLAs for different services. Consider whether these are appropriate for your system. For a mission-critical system, very high availability may be appropriate. For a system that is used for ad-hoc services, a much lower SLA may be appropriate. Consider whether the SLA offered by Azure is a good fit.

---

[24] *http://www.microsoft.com/azure/faq.mspx*

Questions for jeans > The big picture

☒	Question	Why this matters
☐	7.1.12 What would be the impact of a system outage to your business?	Azure provides financially backed SLAs. Consider whether these financial penalties are in line with the impact of a system outage to your business.
☐	7.1.13 What level of raw performance can my application expect from Azure?	Based on the announcement at PDC 08[25], one virtual machine will run 64-bit Windows Server 2008 with CPU equivalent to 1.5-1.7 GHz, 1.7 GB available RAM, 250 GB transient local storage and have a 100 Mbps network. Consider what specification of server you currently use and whether this is fully utilized.
☐	7.1.14 Can the computation run on a low-power server?	The Azure VM is a relatively low-power server. Azure offers the ability to scale out so that you can split your computation across many servers. Some computations run more quickly on one fast server than two slower ones.

---

[25] "Under the Hood: Inside The Cloud Computing Hosting Environment" *http://channel9.msdn.com/pdc2008/ES19/*

Questions for jeans > The big picture

☒	Question	Why this matters
☐	7.1.15 Can the computation time be reduced?	To be able to reduce your computation time using Azure you must be able to use a divide and conquer approach (scale out). This may mean taking a large computation and splitting it up into roughly equal sized independent pieces or using a message based processing style. Microsoft is actively pursuing research in parallel computing which could be applicable to Azure[26]. Certain complex computations cannot be split out this way and can only be sped up by running on faster servers (scale up). Computations such as these are more suited to grid computing platforms such as a Microsoft High Performance Computing.
☐	7.1.16 Are there high performance / low latency requirements within the application?	If your application is going to be a high performance transactional messaging system, you need to carefully consider how Azure could be appropriate. With Azure you may not have the control to throttle or shape network traffic in the same way as you can when you own the infrastructure. Windows Azure Storage data access is based solely on a HTTP RESTful architecture. Consider if this could adversely affect performance for your users or application. Consider what type of data store would be most suitable.

---

[26] "The Dryad Project is investigating programming models for writing parallel and distributed programs to scale from a small cluster to a large data-center" *http://research.microsoft.com/en-us/projects/Dryad/*

Questions for jeans > The big picture

☒	Question	Why this matters
☐	7.1.17 Does the amount of computation required vary?	Azure is particularly suited where the amount of computational capacity varies over time. Azure is highly scalable. Windows Azure enables additional instances of a role to be added extremely rapidly. Consider whether your application requires this behavior.
☐	7.1.18 Do you require massive data storage?	Azure provides the potential for massive data storage. Consider how you will need to access this data. Azure is accessible from anywhere, is this useful? Consider also the overhead of moving large amounts of data to Azure. There might be better solutions for a pure storage requirement.
☐	7.1.19 Do you need to store and manage individual items of data that are very large?	With an on-premises system, clients will be connected to the data repository on an internal (high-speed) network. With Azure, clients connect to the data store over the public Internet. If your system manages large files an Azure application is not necessarily the right choice. It is important to consider performance implications of sending and receiving data within your application.
☐	7.1.20 How does Azure approach scalability requirements?	Azure is built on a massively scalable platform. For applications hosted on Windows Azure, the approach is to scale-out. Consider whether scale-out or scale up is appropriate for your application.

89

Questions for jeans > The big picture

☒	Question	Why this matters
☐	7.1.21 Will Azure solve my application scalability problems?	Taking advantage of the scalability of Azure is very straightforward; it provides a simple mechanism to increase the number of a particular role. It additionally provides queues as a mechanism to distribute work. If your system currently has bottlenecks, Azure is not a silver bullet. If you have an existing system with performance or scalability problems this will not necessarily be fixed by migrating to Azure. Understand your scalability problems and consider whether Azure provides a route to solve these. The Service Management API[27] may assist you with this.
☐	7.1.22 Does Windows Azure support dynamic scale up and scale down for my application?	Consider the usage patterns of your application. Do you have unpredictable periods of load, where dynamic scaling would be useful? Do you have high usage during the day but lower during the night? Windows Azure does not provide any dynamic scaling. While this might offer significant benefits, there is also a high degree of unpredictability in the cost that you will pay. Consider whether this is something that you require and how it would be managed.
☐	7.1.23 Can communication to Azure be secured?	Transport-level security (TLS) is well supported for communication to Azure. Windows Azure storage provides message level authentication with a HMAC SHA256 signature. All SQL Azure communication must be encrypted.

---

[27] *http://blogs.msdn.com/windowsazure/archive/2009/09/17/introducing-the-windows-azure-service-management-api.aspx*

Questions for jeans > The big picture

☒	Question	Why this matters
☐	7.1.24 Are there legal restrictions on how data may be transmitted?	Certain data can only be transmitted over secure networks, such as the N3 network in the UK used by the National Health Service. You cannot connect to any of these networks from within Azure at present.
☐	7.1.25 Can you choose where your data is physically stored?	Consider why you need to know the physical location of your data. How granular is your requirement: country, data center, rack or disk. Azure provides the facility to choose the region where your data is located. Consider whether this granularity matches your needs. Additional geo-location questions can be found in the next section.
☐	7.1.26 What level of physical security does Azure provide?	Many customers need to feel comfortable with the physical security surrounding their servers. Microsoft's Cloud infrastructure achieves both SAS 70 Type I and Type II compliance. The infrastructure program has been independently certified by British Standards Institute (BSI) Management Systems America as being compliant with ISO / IEC 27001:2005[28].

---

[28] "Securing Microsoft's Cloud Infrastructure" *www.globalfoundationservices.com/security/documents/SecuringtheMSCloudMay09.pdf*

Questions for jeans > The big picture

☒	Question	Why this matters
☐	7.1.27 Are there any decisions that might make migrating to Azure in the future easier?	Azure is based on a service oriented architecture. Consider designing your application using this paradigm. Azure web roles are more analogous to web application projects than web site projects in ASP.NET. By using web application projects and developing against IIS 7, you will ease later migrating. Azure currently runs version 3.5 SP1 of the .NET framework. Consider developing against this version.
☐	7.1.28 Can you architect the application to work on-premises and in Azure?	Perhaps you are considering how you might want to migrate off Azure in the future. A common approach might be to use a provider based or pluggable architecture. For instance an ASP.NET provider model or MEF might be useful. Consider whether the additional time, cost and complexity of such an architecture is warranted.

7.2 Design considerations

Beyond the big picture there are a number of more specific questions which you may need to ask.

This section jumps right to the crux of any application. How much is it going to cost? And how can you have it for less? There are a number of questions to help you consider the cost of Azure. In particular, how to design for Azure and whether there is a need for cost oriented architecture.

The second half of this section has questions regarding the global nature of Azure. Where can you use Azure? What time is it in Azure?

This section closes by providing questions to help you consider the limitations that might be presented by Azure. What limitations are there currently in Azure? What restrictions are there for 3rd party services? What issues are there for use of existing components?

Questions for jeans > Design considerations

☒	**Question**	**Why this matters**
☐	7.2.1 Does the pricing model change my solution architecture? Do you need cost oriented architecture?	This is a particularly interesting question. Creating a new architectural approach with "cost oriented architecture" is an interesting notion, but generally a good solution architecture will provide the best long term approach. Model the cost of the Azure services your application will utilize. Consider whether there is anything you can do to reduce these costs without degrading your architecture.
☐	7.2.2 What can you do to reduce the Azure bandwidth cost you pay?	Consider compression e.g. for web role HTTP traffic[29] or messages sent using the .NET Service Bus. When selecting the binding and message format types for services understand their relative bandwidth overhead. However, measure any saving that you might make against the cost of building, testing and supporting the application.
☐	7.2.3 What can you do to reduce the Azure storage cost you pay?	Compression can be used for all types of Azure storage. Consider compressing data before it is stored. However, weigh this against the extra CPU and time required to retrieve and write the data.

---

[29] *http://social.msdn.microsoft.com/Forums/en-US/windowsazure/thread/74900c94-b078-4536-8586-43e795ff5d92*

Questions for jeans > Design considerations

☒	Question	Why this matters
☐	7.2.4 What additionally can you do to reduce the Azure storage cost you pay?	The relative per GB cost of SQL Azure is significantly more than the cost of Windows Azure storage. This is because SQL Azure is a relational database. Often, databases are used to store data that has a limited relational nature. For instance relatively static reference data or configuration data. Consider whether the data you store requires a relational database. It may be possible to migrate to Windows Azure storage[30]. Be aware that you risk sacrificing easy portability of your data and create the need to learn a new technology.
☐	7.2.5 If you definitely need SQL Azure. What additionally can you do to reduce the SQL Azure cost you pay?	SQL Azure has a different pricing model from Windows Azure storage. SQL Azure allows a single database with an upper size limit (1GB or 10GB). Consider how to maximize the storage you buy. Where you have several different databases currently, consider whether these can be stored in fewer databases. However, remember that each database also has a limit on CPU, IO and network bandwidth[31]. This is a potentially significant architectural change and should be considered very carefully.

---

[30] http://www.dotnetsolutions.co.uk/blog/archive/2009/02/24/moving-scrumwall-to-the-windows-azure-platform-(part-1-the-data)/

[31] http://social.msdn.microsoft.com/Forums/en-US/ssdsgetstarted/thread/ac7776ad-0173-448a-8c96-27e418245197/

Questions for jeans > Design considerations

☒	Question	Why this matters
☐	7.2.6 What can you do to reduce the Azure compute cost you pay?	The Windows Azure compute cost is based on the number of VM hours used. Consider the total number of instances you need for each role. Determine whether there are approaches to maximize your VM hours. For example, consider whether a Worker role instance could be used to perform lower priority tasks when it is idle.
☐	7.2.7 When deploying an application to Azure are there any geographical restrictions to be aware of?	Currently Azure is in open CTP. However, after the CTP closes there will be geographical restrictions. There is a list of specific countries where Azure will be available[32]. This list will increase over time.
☐	7.2.8 Are there any geographical restrictions when accessing an application based in Azure?	Microsoft has placed restrictions on the countries where you can deploy an application. However, Microsoft has not placed any restrictions on where you can access an application hosted on Azure. You may want to consider whether there are any restrictions specific to you needs.
☐	7.2.9 Do you need to route users to different applications or different parts of an application based on their country of origin?	One common geo-location approach is to use the client's IP address and effectively lookup the country based on this. Azure does not provide any specific support for this requirement. Nor does it solve any of the common issues associated with proxy servers.

---

[32] http://www.microsoft.com/azure/faq.mspx

Questions for jeans > Design considerations

☒	Question	Why this matters
☐	7.2.10 Do you need to track which user accessed your application and the activities they performed?	Azure will monitor and provide utilization information. However, this will be for your application as a whole. You may also need to track the activity of users to provide data for your own billing system. Consider if there are any requirements on the architecture as a results of the billing strategy.
☐	7.2.11 Do you need to ensure that users store data in a data center in their region?	Azure will have data centers in multiple regions. However, there will not be a data center in every country. Consider whether there are legal restrictions on where data can be stored. Consider also user preferences and how you manage their data. Consider whether your application needs to be able to store data in a particular region. Consider whether your application needs to store data in different regions for different users.
☐	7.2.12 Do you need to ensure your application and database is geo-located?	Consider "code near" or "code far" architecture[33]. "Code near", for example a Windows Azure application with SQL Azure database, has the code and data located close together. "Code far", such as an on-premises application with a SQL Azure database, has the code and data distant from each other. "Code near" architecture will provide your application with best performance and is the most common scenario. Azure provides affinity groups to allow you to create "code near" architecture.

---

[33] "The Relational Database of the Azure Services Platform"
http://msdn.microsoft.com/en-us/magazine/ee321567.aspx

97

Questions for jeans > Design considerations

☒	Question	Why this matters
☐	7.2.13 What is the time in Azure?	Some applications rely on knowing the local time. Perhaps to determine the next date and time to offer an item for delivery. Azure runs in the Coordinated Universal Time (UTC) time zone. Consider whether you need to know the local time for your user. This may be related to questions in 7.2.9 and 7.2.10. Consider whether your application is used in multiple time zones. Consider how to determine the local time. Bear in mind that a simple UTC offset will not account for changes in Daylight Savings Time in the US or British Summer Time in the UK.
☐	7.2.14 Are there any limitations to the type of processing you can do with Windows Azure?	There are essentially no limitations imposed by Windows Azure beyond those of the physical infrastructure. These might include the CPU, IO and bandwidth available to a one VM. Where one instance is not enough, consider your scalability needs. Some questions on this topic are included in 7.1.

Questions for jeans > Design considerations

☒	Question	Why this matters
☐	7.2.15 Are there any limitations to the types of application you can build when using .NET Services?	.NET Services is based on standard REST, SOAP and WS-* techniques. The .NET Services SDK provides WCF bindings. The WCF bindings are provided in a standard .NET framework assembly. Therefore, any project type that can compile this assembly can take advantage of these bindings. However, not all project types can use this assembly. Silverlight, for instance, cannot use these WCF bindings at present. However, REST and SOAP API can be used. However these do not provide the advanced functionality and superior developer experience available with WCF.
☐	7.2.16 Are there any limitations to the type of processing you can do with .NET Service?	There are some limitations imposed in the current CTP[34]. For instance, there is a 60K message size maximum and a limit of 25 active listeners. Message streaming is not supported[35]. These limitations may be removed or updated at a later time. Consider the types of limits you require and match these against those offered by .NET Services.

---

[34] "Microsoft .NET Services July 2009 CTP" *http://msdn.microsoft.com/en-us/library/dd630576.aspx*

[35] "A Developer's Guide to the Microsoft .NET Service Bus" *http://go.microsoft.com/fwlink/?LinkID=150834*

Questions for jeans > Design considerations

☒	Question	Why this matters
☐	7.2.17 Are there are limitations to the type of processing you can do with SQL Azure?	SQL Azure has some limitations. "In order to provide a good experience to all SQL Azure customers, your connection to the service may be closed"[36] in some conditions. These conditions include excessive resource usage and long running queries. It is useful to be aware of these limitations. However, these may also be undesirable behavior for your own application.
☐	7.2.18 Are there any restrictions imposed on consuming (calling out to) 3rd party services from Azure?	Azure allows outbound traffic on all common ports. Although it would be advisable to test any ports you plan to use. More importantly, some 3rd party services use your IP address to grant and restrict access to their services. Azure currently use a DNS naming approach and does not provide an IP address for your application[37]. Consider your requirements when selecting 3rd party service vendors from your application.

---

[36] "Guidelines and Limitations (SQL Azure Database)" *http://msdn.microsoft.com/en-us/library/ee336245.aspx*

[37] "Windows Azure provides a friendly DNS name like "[xxx].cloudapp.net". There's a reason for providing these (other than simply being prettier than an IP address). These are a necessary abstraction layer that lets the Virtual IP addresses (VIPs) underneath change without disrupting your service. It's rare for the VIP of an application to change, but particularly thinking ahead to geo-location scenarios, it's important that Windows Azure reserves the right to change the VIP." *http://blog.smarx.com/posts/custom-domain-names-in-windows-azure*

Questions for jeans > Design considerations

☒	Question	Why this matters
☐	7.2.19 Are there 3rd party component licensing or supported issues relating to Azure?	Azure runs on virtual machines and does not provide a fixed IP address. The details of the machine, e.g. the number of cores, may not be known. Consider checking with any 3rd party component vendors you currently use to determine whether there are any restrictions for use on Azure. Are there restrictions regarding the use of virtual machines? Is there a need to know the physical architecture, e.g. the number of cores? Is the license tied to an IP address?
☐	7.2.20 How does the licensing model work for 3rd party components where the number of instances may scale up and scale down?	Since this model of scalability is fundamental to the architecture of Azure it is important to understand any licensing consequences. Consider checking with any 3rd party component vendors you plan to use to determine whether they have a licensing model for Azure.
☐	7.2.21 Are there any legacy non .NET components that you plan to reuse?	Windows Azure does not provide the ability to "install" third party components. This may mean you are forced to re-write functionality which is freely available within the market at present. Azure does provide the ability to upload legacy COM components and access them from within your application. However, these must conform to COM installation standards. Any that require additional configuration or setup after installation are not supported. Consider whether there are any COM components that you plan to reuse and ensure that they follow best practice advice for native code execution on Azure.

Questions for jeans > Design considerations

☒	Question	Why this matters
☐	7.2.22 What does Azure not do?	Azure does not do everything, nor does it attempt to. There are some common misconceptions about what Azure provides. There are also recurring feature requests. 7.2.23-7.2.25 has some of these questions.
☐	7.2.23 Does Azure manage my domain name?	Azure does not manage your domain name or your DNS entry. This service is still provided by a domain name registrar.
☐	7.2.24 Can you use Azure as a CDN?	At the present time, Azure is not a content delivery network (CDN). Your application and data is served from a specific geo-location.
☐	7.2.25 Does Azure provide an SMTP service?	Azure does not provide an SMTP service. However, there are many internet reachable SMTP services that you could choose to use from Azure.
☐	7.2.26 Can you use your own domain name?	Windows Azure provides a domain name for an application of [app].cloudapp.net; e.g. scrumwall.cloudapp.net. Consider whether you would prefer to use your own domain name for the application. You may want to have consistent branding or remove any association with Azure. This is possible by the use of a CNAME and can be configured through your domain name registrar[38].

---

[38] http://blog.smarx.com/posts/custom-domain-names-in-windows-azure

7.3 Developing for Azure

Developing an application is a complex process. Before beginning there are a number of questions that should be asked to help ensure a successful delivery.

This section begins with a set of developer-centric questions focused on building an application. What programming languages are available? What tools are provided?

The middle part of this section picks up some common questions raised during development. These include storing configuration data, session management and access control.

The latter half of this section provides questions around best practice considerations for Azure. What is the best practice for partitioning data in Windows Azure Table storage? How are transactions managed? How do you build a multi-tenanted application using SQL Azure?

Questions for jeans > Developing for Azure

☒	Question	Why this matters
☐	7.3.1 What programming languages can be used with Windows Azure?	As Windows Azure is a Platform-as-a-Service, it has support for specific languages. Naturally, Azure provides excellent support for .NET framework languages. Windows Azure also provides support for other 3rd party languages via FastCGI. This includes languages such as PHP. Questions have also been asked about Java support[39]. Consider how you are able to use the skills in your development team with Azure.
☐	7.3.2 Are all the features of these programming languages supported by Windows Azure?	By default Windows Azure has a partial trust policy, which prevents certain features. Full trust support can be easily enabled and provides access to most features. However code access security does prevent some operations, such as registry changes[40]. Consider the features that you need to use and whether these are supported by Windows Azure.
☐	7.3.3 What programming languages can be used with .NET Services?	.NET Services offers interoperability by design through industry standards and web protocols such as REST, SOAP, WS-*. In addition, there is a .NET framework SDK provided by Microsoft. There is also a Java SDK and a Ruby SDK provided by partners. Consider which language is most appropriate for you. Consider how support for a non .NET language will be provided by a partner.

---

[39] http://blog.smarx.com/posts/does-windows-azure-support-java

[40] http://blogs.msdn.com/windowsazure/archive/2009/03/18/hosting-roles-under-net-full-trust.aspx

Questions for jeans > Developing for Azure

☒	Question	Why this matters
☐	7.3.4 What tools are your developers familiar with using?	Consider the development tools that your team relies on. The best developer experience for Azure is currently provided by Microsoft's development tools, such as Visual Studio. Microsoft is encouraging other vendors to build tools for Azure. All the functionality is also available from the command line. Consider the tools you would provide to your development team and their cost.
☐	7.3.5 What development environment is available for Windows Azure?	Windows Azure is a Cloud platform; building against a local copy of Windows Azure provides benefits in terms of the speed of development and debugging. Microsoft provides a development fabric for Windows Azure and a development storage utility to simulate Windows Azure Table, Blob and Queue storage. These provide a basis for development of Windows Azure applications. However, the development fabric and storage does behave differently from Windows Azure. Consider how to ensure that you identify any differences for your application early.
☐	7.3.6 What development environment is available for .NET Services?	While a development fabric is provided for Windows Azure, no development platform is available for .NET Services. Consider how you currently develop applications. Consider whether you would need to adapt this approach to allow you to develop directly against .NET Services. Consider whether your developers have guaranteed internet access.

Questions for jeans > Developing for Azure

☒	Question	Why this matters
☐	7.3.7 What development environment is available for SQL Azure?	No development version of SQL Azure is available. SQL Express provides a basic option as a development environment. However, it does not reproduce the features and SQL language limitations of SQL Azure. Consider how you currently work with a development database; do you have one common database or one per developer. Consider how you maintain development databases. Consider whether you would change these approaches for SQL Azure.
☐	7.3.8 Do you have to pay to use Azure while developing and testing an application?	Microsoft will offer, through its MSDN Premium subscription, developers the ability to develop, deploy, and manage multiple Azure applications[41]. Consider whether this option provides a way to reduce the need to pay to use Azure while developing and testing an application.
☐	7.3.9 How do you manage simple configuration settings for an application?	There are essentially two in-built options for managing simple application configuration values. Each role has its own configuration file. Windows Azure also provides a central configuration file. Changes to the Windows Azure configuration file can be made without the need to deploy the application. However changes to the role's configuration require it to be redeployed. Consider what features or options you would need to change. Consider whether redeploying the application is acceptable to change these.

---

[41] http://www.microsoft.com/azure/faq.mspx

Questions for jeans > Developing for Azure

☒	Question	Why this matters
☐	7.3.10 How do you manage more complex configuration settings for an application?	While Windows Azure provides a configuration file it only supports simple string values. The .NET framework provides a much richer configuration file that is available to each role. However changes to this require the role to be redeployed. Consider the level and type of configuration you required for your application. More complex configuration requirements are likely to require custom development.
☐	7.3.11 What is the impact of session state with Windows Azure?	Session state can make building a scalable architecture difficult. Consider whether your application requires session state. Consider whether you can manage without session state, preferring to be stateless[42].
☐	7.3.12 How do you manage session state across multiple Windows Azure instances?	One common workaround is to rely on sticky sessions or server affinity. This ensures that all requests for a session are directed to the same instance. However Window Azure does not support server affinity based load balancing. Web roles can take advantage of the ASP.NET provider model for session state management. However the existing provider may not be appropriate for Azure. A sample Azure session state provider for Table storage is available. Consider how your application will share session state across different instances.

---

[42] "Windows Azure Cloud Service Development Best Practices" *http://channel9.msdn.com/pdc2008/ES03/*

Questions for jeans > Developing for Azure

☒	Question	Why this matters
☐	7.3.13 Does Windows Azure provide any in-built caching capabilities (e.g. for application data) [43]?	Windows Azure does not provide any explicit caching capabilities. However, as an example the ASP.NET cache can be used for web roles. You will need to consider how to manage caching when running multiple instance of a role. Consider how to use dependencies to invalidate a cached object, as file dependency may not be possible.
☐	7.3.14 How do you create a local disk based cache for an application (e.g. for application data)?	Windows Azure provides a local persistent storage on each VM of up to 50GB. However, do not rely on this as your only data store. Consider that your VM may be upgraded or fail and your cache lost. Be prepared to reconstruct any local data[44]. Consider how you would manage building this local cache. Consider how your application would recreate a local cache e.g. on startup.

---

[43] *http://social.msdn.microsoft.com/Forums/en-US/windowsazure/thread/467109ce-9c3f-44eb-bb27-1ebf05e5157d*

[44] "Windows Azure Cloud Service Development Best Practices" *http://channel9.msdn.com/pdc2008/ES03/*

Questions for jeans > Developing for Azure

☒	Question	Why this matters
☐	7.3.15 What options are there for authentication and authorization of users?[45]	The .NET Access Control Service provides a claims based identity model. This can provide access control services for both active (smart client applications) and passive (browser based applications) clients. While the .NET Access Control Service is highly configurable, it is not the only option.. Other options include managing your own access control or delegating to an authentication provider e.g. Windows Live ID. Consider how you plan to authenticate users. Do you have an existing user base? Do you want to provide several authentication options? Consider whether your application has a role based security model. How many roles do you require and how are these managed?
☐	7.3.16 Does the .NET Access Control Service provide integration with Active Directory (AD) and identity providers?	The .NET Access Control Service contains a number of system provided issuers, such as Windows Live ID. The .NET Access Control Service requires a public URI for an identity provider and the certificate used by that identity provider. Active Directory integration is possible using the Geneva Server identity provider[46]. Consider the identity providers are appropriate for your application. Consider whether these providers have a public URI and are compliant with the .NET Access Control Service.

---

[45] *http://blogs.msdn.com/netservices/archive/2009/09/18/update-on-the-next-microsoft-net-services-ctp.aspx*

[46] "A Developer's Guide to the Microsoft .NET Access Control Service" *http://go.microsoft.com/fwlink/?LinkID=150835*

Questions for jeans > Developing for Azure

☒	**Question**	**Why this matters**
☐	7.3.17 Is there any general best practice advice for Windows Azure development?	Consider a loosely coupled architecture for your application. Consider building messaging that is chunky not chatty for communication between different parts of your application. Consider using asynchronous processing of messages and do this in an idempotent way.[47]
☐	7.3.18 How are transactions managed by Windows Azure storage?	Windows Azure Table storage provides entity group transactions. This supports batch transactions within a single table and for a single partition within that table. Consider what type of transactional operations you need to perform. Does it involve multiple partitions, multiple tables? Does it involve a data store outside Azure? Consider whether you can build a mechanism to manage transactions. Consider whether SQL Azure would be a better option to handle more complex transactional requirements.

---

[47] "Windows Azure Cloud Service Development Best Practices" *http://channel9.msdn.com/pdc2008/ES03/*

Questions for jeans > Developing for Azure

☒	Question	Why this matters
☐	7.3.19 Is there any guidance or best practice for partitioning data in Windows Azure Table storage?	The way in which data is partitioned can have a significant impact on the scalability and performance of an application. The scalability is improved by having multiple partitions. This allows the query load to be distributed. However, the performance benefits of a query constrained to a single partition can be significant for a large table. Entity group transactions can be used only where all entities are in the same partition. Consider how the data will be used. It may be appropriate to hold multiple copies of the data; each copy partitioned differently and optimized for a particular set of queries. However, when duplicating data consider how to maintain consistency across multiple copies.
☐	7.3.20 Do Windows Azure Queues provide a strict first-in-first-out (FIFO) queue?	When developing with Windows Azure Queues have awareness that they do not strictly guaranteed message order. When a message is read from the queue it is not removed. Instead it is marked as invisible for a certain time. Therefore, particularly under high load, it is possible that a message will be read more than once. Consider how to provide idempotent processing of a message.

☒	Question	Why this matters
☐	7.3.21 Is there any additional best practice advice available for Windows Azure Tables, Blobs and Queues?	General best practice advice is beyond the scope of the book. However, there are white papers available for Windows Azure Table, Windows Azure Blob and Windows Azure Queue storage.[48] These contain a more in-depth examination of the questions raised in this section. They also each contain a specific best practice section.
☐	7.3.22 When using the .NET Service Bus, which binding should you use?	The .NET Service Bus offers multiple bindings. "The TCP relay binding is the binding of choice in the majority of cases involving relayed Internet connectivity. It yields the best performance and throughput while minimizing the overhead for both the service and the relay service. It supports request-reply operations, one-way operations, and even duplex callbacks, all through the relay service."[49] Consider the type of operations that you need to do, the performance required and whether any firewall changes are required.

---

[48] http://www.microsoft.com/azure/whitepaper.mspx

[49] "Working With The .NET Service Bus" http://msdn.microsoft.com/en-us/magazine/dd569756.aspx

Questions for jeans > Developing for Azure

☒	Question	Why this matters
☐	7.3.23 Is there any firewall change required to connect to the .NET Service Bus?	This depends on the type of binding used by the system. Some require TCP ports 808, 818, 819, and 828 to be opened for outbound traffic[50]. These may not be open on your firewall by default. However, other bindings relay messages over port 80 or 443. These ports are generally open by default. Consider your ability to make firewall changes and the benefits of the different bindings.
☐	7.3.24 What standards does the .NET Access Control Service adhere to?[51]	The .NET Access Control Service is WS-Trust 1.3 compliant and creates SAML (Security Assertion Markup Language) compliant security tokens. Consider the identity provider that you would use and the standards it supports.
☐	7.3.25 How are transactions managed by SQL Azure?	SQL Azure provides full transactional support within a single database. However, there is no support for distributed queries or transactions. Consider how you would manage transactions within SQL Azure or within your application. Consider whether you need to perform distributed transactions within SQL Azure database or with on-premises systems.

---

[50] "Service Bus Connectivity Service" http://msdn.microsoft.com/en-us/library/dd582710.aspx

[51] http://blogs.msdn.com/netservices/archive/2009/09/18/update-on-the-next-microsoft-net-services-ctp.aspx

Questions for jeans > Developing for Azure

☒	Question	Why this matters
☐	7.3.26 How do you build a multi-tenanted application using SQL Azure?	SQL Azure has the raw capability to support large scale multi-tenanted applications. It also has the ability to provision new databases far more rapidly that a traditional on-premises solution. SQL Azure does not fundamentally change multi-tenant data architecture. However, it does provide a compelling reason to examine your data architecture. Consider the number, nature, and needs of your tenants when selecting the most appropriate tenant model[52]. Also consider the SQL Azure database size limitations and the cost implications for each model.
☐	7.3.27 Does SQL Azure support partitioning of data?	The business edition of SQL Azure currently has the largest size limit, 10GB. This limit is for the database as a whole and includes indexes as well as data. Consider whether your application breaches this limit. SQL Azure does not provide any support for partitioning of data. Consider using a data sharding technique to store data in multiple databases. However, you will need to manage referential integrity of the data across these databases yourself. Consider whether sharding provides a reasonable option and the cost of managing this process for your application.

---

[52] "Multi-Tenant Data Architecture" *http://msdn.microsoft.com/en-us/library/aa479086.aspx*

Questions for jeans > Developing for Azure

☒	Question	Why this matters
☐	7.3.28 Does SQL Azure support data mining, reporting or replication?	Analysis Services, Replication, Reporting Services, and Service Broker are not currently provided. There is currently no specific support in Azure for data mining. However, the SQL Server Data Mining team is working in this area and has previously built a prototype[53].

---

[53] "Data Mining in the Cloud" *http://www.microsoft.com/azure/mining.mspx*

115

7.4 Application lifecycle management

There is more to delivering a successful application than coding. There are questions that should be asked regarding testing, deployment and operational needs. The focus of this section is on the second half of the application lifecycle and also includes operational considerations.

This section opens with questions pertaining to the second half of the application lifecycle. Do you need a new application lifecycle management tool? How do you build test and preproduction environments for Azure? How do you perform an upgrade in Azure?

A series of questions covering operational and support considerations follow. How do you debug Windows Azure? Can you access server logs? What level of health monitoring is available in Azure? How are security patches applied by the fabric controller?

This section closes by offering questions that cover backup, audit, archiving and data retention. How do you backup data in Azure? What audited functionality is available?

Questions for jeans > Application lifecycle management

☒	Question	Why this matters
☐	7.4.1 Do you have an application lifecycle management tool you currently use?	Consider your current source control, continuous integration and software build requirements. Azure projects have a number of new file extension types, which may require changes to your tool configuration. Consider whether you need a make any modification to your source control management. Where you do not currently have an ALM tool, consider whether now offers an opportunity to use one. Consider how you use continuous integration and what support is offered for this by Azure.
☐	7.4.2 Do my development and support teams need to learn a whole new set of skills and technologies?	Certainly there will be aspects of Azure that will require new skills. However, Azure development is well supported for .NET developers with a number of SDKs. Windows Azure provides support for familiar technologies including LINQ, ADO.NET data services and REST. .NET Services is based on standard REST, SOAP and WS-* techniques. SQL Azure supports a subset of familiar T-SQL. Consider the overlap between your current skills and those required for Azure development. Consider what training is available for these technologies or specifically for Azure.

Questions for jeans > Application lifecycle management

☒	Question	Why this matters
☐	7.4.3 Do you need to create tools for my internal commercial team that provide usage and billing information?	Azure provides an administration and billing platform. This provides billing information for your application as a whole. Consider whether this is acceptable or whether a more detailed level of information is required by your commercial team. Consider how you would expose and report this information. Consider also the languages used by your team. The administration portal is currently available in English; however, more languages may be added.
☐	7.4.4 Do you need to create tools for my customers to provide usage and billing information?	This Azure administration portal will provide usage and billing information. However you may want to limit direct access to the portal where you have multiple tenants or you are providing a service. Consider the requirements of your customers. Do they need up-to-date or "near real time" usage information? Do they require predictive billing information based on trends or part month usage? Consider how you would architect your multi-tenanted application to capture this information. Consider how you would create a tool to offer this information to your customers.

Questions for jeans > Application lifecycle management

☒	Question	Why this matters
☐	7.4.5 How many test and preproduction environments do you envisage needing?	Consider your current testing and operational processes. How many different environments do you currently use? A Windows Azure solution provides two environments; staging and live. However .NET Services and SQL Azure do not provide a staging environment. While there is no specific support, additional environments can be constructed by simply creating another solution. Consider the potential cost of running and maintaining multiple environments in Azure.
☐	7.4.6 How do you undertake integration testing?	One of the aims of integration testing is to verify the required performance of an application. Therefore it is vital to use a test environment that can be equated to the production environment. Consider how you will measure your integration testing. Consider whether there is a cost associated with running integration testing on Azure with a high transaction load.
☐	7.4.7 How do you undertake system testing?	Different aspects of system testing may be managed in parallel or on a single test environment. Consider how you currently manage system testing. Do you rely on using a closed network where all components can behave as if live? With Azure your test environment cannot, for instance, have the same URL as your live environment. Consider whether your application or testing procedures relies on mimicking the live environment. Consider also how this impacts user acceptance testing.

Questions for jeans > Application lifecycle management

☒	Question	Why this matters
☐	7.4.8 Do you undertake stress or destructive testing?	Stress testing is aimed at testing an application beyond its normal load, often to breaking point. The purpose being to understand the behavior of the application in extremes and whether it can recover when load is reduced. Generally this type of testing involves monitoring server and network performance. However, this type of monitoring is not supported by Azure. Be aware that this type of testing may be mistaken for a denial of service attack. Where your application has been designed to scale automatically, stress testing may just create more instances. Consider your need to undertake such testing. Consider whether such testing is permitted under the Azure licensing agreement.
☐	7.4.9 Do you undertake penetration testing or ethical hacking as part of your test program?	Security or vulnerability testing is undertaken generally at the application level, e.g. cross-site scripting. Penetration testing or ethical hacking is aimed at both software and hardware faults. Consider whether you have a legal or contractual requirement to perform this type of testing. Consider whether such testing is permitted under the Azure licensing agreement.

Questions for jeans > Application lifecycle management

☒	Question	Why this matters
☐	7.4.10 How do you build test and preproduction environments?	Consider how you currently build a new environment: the application, the data etc. Environment (VM) cloning and database backup / restore are traditional techniques used to speed up environment creation. However, neither of these techniques is available in Azure. Consider how you would setup a test environment in Azure. Understand the time, cost and complexity for this undertaking. Consider whether you need to change your testing approach.
☐	7.4.11 How do you perform an initial deployment to Azure?	The physical deployment of an application to Windows Azure is relatively simple. With Windows Azure storage it is best practice to ensure that you create the structures required for Blob, Queue and Table first and not as part of a first try read or write. Consider the different Azure services that you plan to use and any dependencies.

Questions for jeans > Application lifecycle management

☒	**Question**	**Why this matters**
☐	7.4.12 How do you perform an upgrade in Azure?	Consider the approach you currently use for application upgrade. Do you have a maintenance window to take down the application or data store? Do you need to perform in-place upgrades? Both options are supported by Azure and there are some general considerations that apply. The best practice advice is to update the code and data separately[54]. This allows for a more controlled upgrade. Ensure that the code, data and potentially both are backwards and forwards compatible. Be aware that there is no simple rollback or restore approach for data in Azure. There are some additional considerations for Azure Table storage[55]. Consider planning your upgrade strategy early.

---

[54] "Windows Azure Cloud Service Development Best Practices" *http://channel9.msdn.com/pdc2008/ES03/*

[55] "Programming Table Storage" *http://go.microsoft.com/fwlink/?LinkId=153401*

Questions for jeans > Application lifecycle management

☒	Question	Why this matters
☐	7.4.13 How do you debug Windows Azure?	The local development fabric allows local debugging. However, it is not possible to debug Windows Azure. A recommended approach is to use logging to output debug information. The use of a unique identifier to connect a task performed across different parts of the application may also be useful as part of the log message.[56] Consider how you currently track down a bug in a live application. Will you need to consider alternatives for Azure? Will you need to provide additional logging information or tools to the support team?
☐	7.4.14 What level of health monitoring is available in Azure?	Consider your current health monitoring processes. When you have physical access to the servers, you can access CPU utilization, memory usage etc which may be useful to detect performance bottlenecks. Windows Azure does not provide direct access to the VM. The Windows Azure fabric controller monitors the health of the VM and the role it runs. A role can also report its health status; this can be configured in code. If there is a failure the fabric controller creates a new VM instance. Consider whether you would need to access server information and how this might be possible in Azure.

---

[56] "Windows Azure Cloud Service Development Best Practices" *http://channel9.msdn.com/pdc2008/ES03/*

Questions for jeans > Application lifecycle management

☒	Question	Why this matters
☐	7.4.15 What diagnostic information might be available if my VM fails?	The Windows Azure fabric controller is responsible for health monitoring and creating a new instance if one fails. An instance might fail for a number of reasons outside of your control, e.g. a hardware fault. However a failure might be due to your application. Consider whether your application is currently experiencing unexpected failures. Windows Azure is not likely to offer a panacea.
☐	7.4.16 Can you access server logs?	Consider whether you require access to server logs. Server logs can sometimes be useful to track down application errors. Consider whether you require access to IIS logs. IIS logs can be used to analyze application usage e.g. requests that returned a page not found response. Windows Azure does not currently provide access to server logs. Consider whether external site monitoring tools provide an alternative. Consider whether you need to create your own additional logging.

Questions for jeans > Application lifecycle management

☒	Question	Why this matters
☐	7.4.17 How does your business deal with regular maintenance?	One of the major benefits of Windows Azure is the management of system and security patches. Upgrades are done by updating one "update domain" at a time. Where you have two instances, these are placed in different "update domains". Consider whether your business require notice for these patches. If you have only one instance, will small periods of outage be acceptable? Will small periods of reduced failover or performance (e.g. where perhaps one of your instances is being patched) be acceptable? Determine whether the patching approaches available with Windows Azure match your business needs.
☐	7.4.18 What application management processes do you have?	Consider your current application management processes. Do you have a firebreak between development, testing, production and commercial functions? Consider how the separation of roles within the Azure administration portal matches your processes. Consider whether you will require additional internal processes for Azure.
☐	7.4.19 How will access to the Azure administration portal be controlled and audited?	This is related to your application management processes. Consider whether you have regulatory or contractual requirements to audit actions made through the Azure administration portal. Consider whether these requirements match the features provided by the portal.

Questions for jeans > Application lifecycle management

☒	Question	Why this matters
☐	7.4.20 How will access to data stored in Azure be controlled and audited?	All access to Windows Azure storage is made with the same credentials and provides full access to the data. No feature to audit access to Windows Azure storage is provided. SQL Azure allows user logins with different permissions to be setup. However, SQL Azure does not support audit. Consider whether you have regulatory or contractual requirements to audit access to data stored in Azure. Consider whether these requirements match the features provided by either Windows Azure storage or SQL Azure.
☐	7.4.21 How do you backup data in Azure?	Neither Windows Azure storage nor SQL Azure provides backup functionality. This is partly due to the fact that data is replicated three times to provide resilience. Data can be copied using other tools or processes, but these would need to be developed. Consider your current backup strategy. Consider whether your data backup is purely to provide resilience or whether it serves other purposes.
☐	7.4.22 If there is a logic flaw in the application or a user makes a serious mistake. How do you rollback changes to data?	Azure does not provide data backup or change tracking. Consider your business process for undoing changes. In order to support rollback, you will need to create a change log and tools to use this. Consider the risks of such an issue to your business. Consider whether you might need to change your process to mitigate the need for a rollback function.

Questions for jeans > Application lifecycle management

☒	Question	Why this matters
☐	7.4.23 How would your system need to recover from a service outage?	Azure provides resilience for its data stores and queues by replicating data. Windows Azure role resilience is provided by the fabric controller. Where your system contains non-Azure components, such as in-house services or desktop applications consider whether this recovery model matches. Do you need to perform any manual verification steps? Do you need to restart services or applications?
☐	7.4.24 How do you manage data retention?	Some applications have explicit data retention rules. Other applications having no explicit requirements and implicitly retain all data. Understand how long and what data will need to be retained. Evaluate the impact of this on your storage requirements. While Windows Azure storage provides unlimited capacity, currently SQL Azure has a 10GB limit for a single database. Depending on the type of Azure storage used, data retention may become a limiting factor. Consider whether your data retention rules can be satisfied by the Azure storage your application will use.

Questions for jeans > Application lifecycle management

☒	Question	Why this matters
☐	7.4.25 Do you require an archiving function for your data retention rules?	Azure does not provide any out-of-the-box archiving features. Consider what type of Azure storage is appropriate for your archived data. Consider whether you want or need to move archives outside Azure. Consider also the purpose of archiving data. Will you need to restore or retrieve this data in the future? How will you manage this process with Azure?
☐	7.4.26 Do you need to purge data when it reaches the period defined by data retention rules?	Azure does not provide any specific features for this requirement. You will need to consider whether an automated or manual approach is more appropriate. In either case, you will need to create this process. This process may also have implications for archiving of data.

Chapter 8

Funny you should say that

Laughter gives us distance. It allows us to step back from an event, deal with it and then move on.

Bob Newhart (Comedian, 1929 –)

WE trust that the previous chapters of questions have been useful and started your thought processes. However if we are honest they can hardly be described as a fun read. What the book is missing are some stories or anecdotes which bring the Smart Questions to life.

Over the following pages we have included stories from the community of Azure early adopters. If we'd interspersed these case studies with the questions it would have made the last chapters too long. It would also have prevented you using the questions as checklists or aide-memoires. So we've grouped them together in this chapter.

Funny you should say that

Case Study: FullArmor

"Azure is a game-changer. Software development becomes more efficient, and the cost of delivering software to customers is reduced by an order of magnitude."

FULLARMOR.
The Leaders in Enterprise Policy Management

Danny Kim, CTO, FullArmor

http://www.fullarmor.com

Clouds forming - drivers to migrate

PolicyPortal, was originally developed in 2005 to help organizations manage and protect PCs both inside and outside Active Directory domains. The application designed with tools and technologies from Microsoft generated a lot of interest from customers. However, the solution was designed to be hosted, so it took a long time to set up with hosting service providers. This led to higher infrastructure costs and delays in closing agreements with customers.

"We did not want to get into the hosting business ourselves, and there were elements of the solution that were too complex to deliver to generic hosting providers." says Kim. "What we really needed was a Cloud-based platform to simplify application delivery, but at the time Cloud computing was still in its infancy. So we decided to sit on the technology and see what would develop."

Cloud cover - the Azure solution

FullArmor became an early adopter of the Windows Azure Platform and started work on the new version of PolicyPortal in mid-2008. It took less than two months to migrate the existing application to the Windows Azure Platform. "We were able to move the application quickly because our original version of PolicyPortal was written in managed code using ASP.NET. As a result, about 80 percent of the code could be migrated without any changes being required in order to work in the Azure environment," says Kim.

Several African countries are now working to deploy PolicyPortal along with a program to supply new laptops to teachers. With the goal to reach hundreds of thousands of teachers, this program, that is designed to elevate the quality of education through the use of technology, would have been cost prohibitive to implement without the scale and cost savings inherent with cloud computing.

Sunny spells - the benefits

FullArmor used the Windows Azure Platform to create a highly flexible and scalable Web-based application that is easy to deploy and manage. Because of the open Internet standards used in the platform, PolicyPortal can operate with a range of devices and non-Windows® operating systems. By adopting the Windows Azure Platform, FullArmor can take advantage of its previous development efforts and extend them to Cloud-based computing.

Provides high flexibility and scalability. "With Azure, we can get our product to market faster, and our customers can enjoy the benefits of PolicyPortal sooner." says Kim.

Interoperates with a range of technologies. Azure provides the ability to create connected Internet applications regardless of the platform with which developers are working. This means that we can deploy PolicyPortal in mixed-enterprise environments."

Extends investment in development work. "We took a traditional IT application and moved it to Azure with very little pain," says Kim. "the Cloud becomes an extension of the enterprise IT environment."

This case study is based on a Microsoft case study that can be found at
http://www.microsoft.com/casestudies/Case_Study_Detail.aspx?CaseStudyID=4000002890

Funny you should say that

Case Study: PensionDCisions

"The Windows Azure platform provides a robust and scalable global opportunity. By extending our on-premises based solution into the cloud we can now address a global market without the infrastructure issues normally associated with so doing."

Richard Burrill, CTO

PensionDCisions®

http://www.pensiondcisions.com

Clear skies - life was fine before the Cloud

PensionDCisions is an innovative young company that uses leading business intelligence (BI) solutions to calculate and benchmark performance for individuals and corporations with defined contribution pensions. Uniquely, PensionDCisions views the behavior and results of each individual scheme member rather than the traditional industry focus on investment products. The metrics are easy to understand and meaningful. PensionDCisions won the European Pension awards Technology Provider of the Year 2009 award with their solution. This functionality was provided by an on-premises Microsoft SQL Server™ 2005 BI reporting suite, including Microsoft SQL Server 2005 Reporting Services and Microsoft SQL Server 2005 Analysis Services.

Clouds forming - drivers to migrate

PensionDCisions utilized an on-premises based solution to provide the aggregation of this data due to the highly customized nature of the SQL Server installation that was required. The market that the firm wanted to make this data available to was, however, hugely diverse. An on-premises based solution was not appropriate as a platform to disseminate this information. This was because it would be placed under varying loads from a global audience. What PensionDCisions needed was a worldwide platform with which they could vary the amount of compute capacity available on the fly. They chose the Windows Azure Platform.

Cloud cover - the Azure solution

Microsoft's vision of Software plus Services is that solutions will continue to be a combination of on-premises and cloud-based assets. This fitted well as PensionDCisions could continue to use their investment in on-premises based data processing and storage solutions whilst augmenting it with the Windows Azure Platform to provide "elastic" distribution to their users. The raw data continues to be aggregated and stored on-premises, then alongside this a series of Azure based applications have been built which allow users to visualize and interact with this data.

Sunny spells - the benefits

The Windows Azure platform has allowed PensionDCisions to reach audiences with ease. It will allow their insights to be presented to a global audience without the infrastructure challenges traditionally associated with so doing. Finally, it has allowed PensionDCisions to vary the compute capacity available as required – avoiding the large up-front capital expenditure which would be required to buy enough servers to deal with spikes in demand.

Funny you should say that

Case Study: Dot Net Solutions

"The Windows Azure platform provided us with the ability to launch an innovative software product to a global user base without the up-front capital expenditure that would otherwise be required."

Dan Scarfe, CEO   http://www.dotnetsolutions.co.uk

Clear skies - life was fine before the Cloud

Dot Net Solutions is a system integrator based in the United Kingdom. As a Microsoft Gold Certified partner, the company uses an agile SCRUM software development methodology to accommodate changing business requirements and prioritize the delivery of defect-free products. To facilitate collaboration between off-site developers and customers, Dot Net developed an electronic ScrumWall for internal use. The application uses the Microsoft Silverlight browser plug-in to create a virtual project wall with notes that can be manipulated on-screen.

Clouds forming - drivers to migrate

The application was a success within the company and garnered interest from the company's customers. Because of this, Dot Net Solutions considered marketing the application as a hosted service. The challenge was that to launch a hosted service would have required a large investment in hardware and support staff. The worst scenario would be for customers to have a substandard experience because of an under-specified infrastructure. The alternative was risking wasting huge amounts of money on hardware and resources that might go unused.

Cloud cover - the Azure solution

The company found its answer in the Windows Azure Platform from Microsoft, an Internet-based operating system that serves as a development, service hosting, and service management environment. The solution is hosted in Microsoft data centers and provides developer services to create flexible, cost-effective solutions. Windows Azure removes all of the headaches of managing the operating system and allowed Dot Net Solutions to focus on their core capability – designing great software experiences for users.

Sunny spells - the benefits

Dot Net Solutions used the Windows Azure Platform to bring a new product to market without a risky capital investment, allowing the company to safely foray into new territory that may hold high revenue potential. The launch required minimal effort due to the easy migration of code to the new environment. The investment costs were substantially reduced by eliminating the need for an on premises infrastructure for ScrumWall. Most importantly, because Windows Azure provides automated service management, the company did not have to hire additional support staff.

This case study is based on a Microsoft case study that can be found at
http://www.microsoft.com/casestudies/Case_Study_Detail.aspx?CaseStudyID=4000004847

Funny you should say that

Case Study: ADXSTUDIO Inc

"By hosting their website in Azure, the newly-formed XRM Virtual User Group avoided up-front capital expenditures and operates with the assurance that future capacity needs will be available on-demand."

Doug Schneider, President

adxstudio

http://www.adxstudio.com

Clear skies - life was fine before the Cloud

ADXSTUDIO has a long-standing history of providing leading edge web content management solutions for the Microsoft platform and this history, experience, and expertise is evident in the design and functionality of their ADXSTUDIO xRM Extensions software. This innovative product helps organizations significantly reduce the time and effort needed to integrate their web portals with the relationship management capabilities of the Microsoft Dynamics™ CRM platform.

Clouds forming - drivers to migrate

As a strong proponent of xRM development, ADXSTUDIO teamed up with the like-minded owners of Colorado Technology Consultants, Inc., who share a desire to promote the virtues of xRM technology and best practices with the development community. Together they concluded that a virtual user group would be the best way to reach their geographically dispersed audience. With a limited budget for advertising, the partners decided to take advantage of the gathering of CRM/xRM-minded people at an upcoming Microsoft Convergence Conference by exhibiting and demonstrating a user group portal. The challenge was to get a site designed, developed, and live in less than two weeks.

Cloud cover - the Azure solution

The solution involved creating a fully-functioning, interactive user group portal (www.xrmvirtual.com) that offered profile and membership management, events, content management, and forum functionality. This web solution was built with the ADXSTUDIO xRM SDK and xRM CMS which leverage Dynamics™ CRM as the underlying development platform and the portal is hosted in Windows Azure. The development team was able to start working directly with no lag for setting up and configuring servers.

Sunny spells - the benefits

The speed with which the Windows Azure and CRM Online instances were provisioned, coupled with the rapid development capabilities of the CRM platform and ADXSTUDIO xRM Extensions, allowed the team to get the portal running in time for the conference. By avoiding up-front capital expenditures for infrastructure this non-profit user group was able to deliver an outstanding web solution on a limited budget. As the interest in the XRM Virtual User Group continues to grow and additional capacity is required to meet peak demands the user group leaders can simply adjust the performance they desire from the Azure infrastructure and only pay for their actual usage.

Funny you should say that

Chapter 9

Time for Action

The world is a dangerous place, not because of those who do evil, but because of those who look on and do nothing.

Albert Einstein (Scientist, 1879 – 1955)

THE stated goal of this book was to provide the Smart Questions that allow you to consider the implications, risks and opportunities of Azure. If, having read the book, your informed decision is that Azure is not right for you, then great. We can take comfort that we have helped prevent you from wasting time and money. We would however encourage you to keep revisiting this decision. The Cloud world is changing and evolving rapidly and the reasons for you staying away today may be resolved more rapidly than you expected.

On the other hand, you may now be excited about the opportunities that Azure offers you and your customers. You may be asking yourself "what next?". This book was never intended to be a "how to guide", however we can provide some pointers to things that could help you get started.

This list is not exhaustive and there will certainly be new resources from both Microsoft and other 3rd parties coming out all the time. We wish you all the best and trust that you will enjoy exploring the possibilities that Azure enables.

- Sign up for an Azure account (*www.azure.com*)
- Talk to you account manager
- Attend awareness and technical sessions
- Consider whether other Microsoft partners can help

Time for Action

- Look at sample code, quick start tutorials and "how to" guides
- See if there is a local Azure User Group
- Talk to your customers
- Consider if there are ways to enhance your existing applications
- Look at the TCO and ROI if you did move to Azure
- Go back and read the questions again

If you have experiences with Azure that you wish to share then send them to *stories@Smart-Questions.com*, we may be able to include them in the next version of the book.

Chapter 10

Appendix - References

Copy from one, it's plagiarism; copy from two, it's research.
Wilson Mizner (Playwright, 1876 – 1933)

As always when putting a book like this together, there are many sources of information that you come across as part of the research. Some of these provide confirmation of existing ideas. Others, put bluntly, are a distraction at best and in reality a waste of valuable time. However across all the hours of research there are certain articles, papers, and blogs that have proved genuinely useful.

In some cases these information sources provide a background to a subject area that we only touch on within this book and yet it would be useful for the reader to have access to deeper coverage.

There are also resources provided by others that can help the reader as they progress from "Thinking of…" to action.

So rather than keep all these references locked away in our heads we offer them here.

Our caveat is that we cannot promise that the pages linked to will still be there when you go to them, or that you will find them as interesting as we did, although we hope that you too will find them helpful.

Appendix - References

General Cloud References

Description	Link
Security Guidance from the Cloud Security Alliance	http://www.cloudsecurityalliance.org/csaguide.pdf
Securing Microsoft's Cloud Infrastructure	http://www.globalfoundationservices.com/security/documents/SecuringtheMSCloudMay09.pdf

Windows Azure Platform References

Description	Link
Azure FAQ	http://www.microsoft.com/azure/faq.mspx
Azure Whitepapers	http://www.microsoft.com/azure/whitepaper.mspx
Introducing Windows Azure	http://www.davidchappell.com/writing/white_papers/Introducing_Windows_Azure_v1-Chappell.pdf
An Introduction to .NET Services for Developers	http://go.microsoft.com/fwlink/?LinkID=150833

Developer Resources

Description	Link
Developer SDK	http://www.microsoft.com/azure/sdk.mspx
Training Kit	http://www.microsoft.com/azure/trainingkit.mspx
"Geneva" Framework Whitepaper for Developers	http://download.microsoft.com/download/7/d/0/7d0b5166-6a8a-418a-addd-95ee9b046994/GenevaFrameworkWhitepaperForDevelopers.pdf

Appendix - References

Best Practice Information

Description	Link
Programming Table Storage	*http://go.microsoft.com/fwlink/?LinkId=153401*
Programming Blob Storage	*http://go.microsoft.com/fwlink/?LinkId=153400*
Programming Queue Storage	*http://go.microsoft.com/fwlink/?LinkId=153402*
Windows Azure: Cloud Service Development Best Practice	*http://channel9.msdn.com/pdc2008/ES03*
.NET and ADO.NET Data Service Performance Tips for Windows Azure Tables	*http://social.msdn.microsoft.com/Forums/en-US/windowsazure/thread/d84ba34b-b0e0-4961-a167-bbe7618beb83*

Notes pages

Notes pages